P9-AFD-869

RENEWALS 458-4574

DATE DUE

| APR 17 | | | |
|--------|--|--|--|
| | | | |
| | | | |
| | | | |
| | | | |
| | | | |
| | | | |
| | | | |
| | | | |
| | | | |
| | | | |
| | | | |
| | | | |
| | | | |
| | | | |
| | | | |
| | | | |
| GAYLORD | | | PRINTED IN U.S.A. |

# LAST
# WORDS

Cover design by Bill Toth
Book design by Iris Bass
Cover art courtesy of the author
Author photograph by Jeff Poniewaz

# LAST
# WORDS
# ANTLER

AVAILABLE
PRESS

BALLANTINE BOOKS • NEW YORK

————————————

**For Jeff Poniewaz**
**Poet, Inspirer, Camerado**

# Contents

# REWORKING WORK

# CATCHING THE SUNRISE

# Acknowledgments

Abraxas
Action
Alemantschen—a Journal of Radical Ecology (Switzerland)
Ambrosia
American Poetry Review
Androgyne
Baltimore Sun
Beatniks From Space
Beloit Poetry Journal
Between the Species
Big Scream
Birthstone
Blake Times
Blow
Blueline
Bombay Gin
Brahma
Brewing: 20 Milwaukee Poets
Bugle American
Changing Men
Chelsea
City 9 (International Writers Anthology)
City Lights Journal #4
CoEvolution Quarterly
Colorado North Review
Coyote's Dance
Crazy Shepherd
Cream City Review
Delirium
Dreamworks
Earth First!
Express
Friction
Ganymede

Gathering Place of the Waters: 30 Milwaukee Poets
Gay Sunshine
Greenfield Review
Hanging Loose
Ironwood
James White Review
Jump River Review
Kyoto Review (Japan)
Lips
Long Shot
Magical Blend
Michigan Voice
Mickle Street Review
Milwaukee Journal
Milwaukee Magazine
Minnesota Review
Nambla
New Blood
New Directions Anthology #37
New Poetry Out of Wisconsin
New York Quarterly
Nightsun
North Country Anvil
O.ars
Pantheist Vision
Passaic Review
Planet Detroit
Plumbers Ink
Poetry Flash
Poetry San Francisco
RFD
Rocky Ledge
San Francisco Sunday Examiner-Chronicle
Sing Heavenly Muse!

Tempest
The Body Politic (Toronto)
The Penis Mighter
The Shepherd
The World
Third Coast Archives
This Book Has No Title
Total Abandon

Wind
Windfall
Wisconsin Poets Calendar (1982,
  1983, 1984)
WisconsIn Step
Woodland Pattern Dial-a-Poem
Wordworks
Zero

The author wishes to thank the Milwaukee Artists Foundation for a grant to work on the poems in "ReWorking Work."

# LAST
# WORDS

# Trying to Remember What I Learned

The old classroom is alone in me
Trying to remember what I learned.
Desktops wrinkled with words.
Under the seats, fingerprints of gum.
Pen on the floor, tip finely chewed.
Listen for the echo of milkteeth.
Not even the janitor
With his broom and red sawdust
Stands here in the middle of night.
Ropes of shades are tied in delicate nooses.
The clock ticks in a circle
Of ages I once was.
This building's a stone
Names wander in and out of,
Laughing when they find their name
The same as the name in a book.
The globe is dark. I used to spin it
And let my finger find where I was going.
The blackboard is clean,
No streaks where moist sponges passed over.
Erasers rest in their troughs,
Thick with white chalk dust.
In one eraser more knowledge
Than hundreds of books?
The chalk rubs off on my fingers
Minute fossilized creatures
That lived millions of years ago.
The fire escape has never been used.
I had to learn all these words.

## Iceboat

Once, in winter, when light left the lake,
Skating far out, a kite made from an old sheet
As my sail, the wind held its breath and listened,
Echoing my ears, and I lay still while clouds
Glaciered my eyes, and I fell through myself
Like a car through thin ice
From which squirmed an old man to the surface
Already frozen over, where skates grinned
And young eyes peered down at the frantic statue.

Standing, I saw across the drifting sky,
Dressed like an Eskimo, small as a spider,
Distant at the shore, pushing his iceboat windward,
My father. How small and warm he was.
I heard the runners groaning. "Come back."
He was so far away I heard his voice
After his mouth had spoken.
Under me I felt the long heart-attack—
Sheets of ice straining toward the bank.
Through me he breathed: "It's cold."
Wind filled the sail and his boat was gone.

"That fish frozen in ice—it's not dead,
With the spring thaw it will swim alive."
He said that once, and we bet when the ice would break.

Swallowing the flakes that melted on my cheeks
I carved my name with my blades, and left
The sail bags for him to bring.
Inside, my mother stood behind cocoa
And I unlaced the guillotines from my feet.

# Rexroth as He Appeared to Exist
## March 24, 1968 9:00 P.M.

It was as if he were slowly falling asleep,
Sitting in that chair, while everyone at the party
      asked him questions.
Suddenly I wondered if someday I'd become a bard
And if, as they asked me questions,
        I'd tilt back my head and for a minute or so
        pretend to doze, eyes peering under lids,
And I wondered if then, in that future crowd,
There'd be anyone like me who once
      couldn't think of any questions to ask,
And couldn't help but think: how soon
      he will be dead
And that's how he'll look in the coffin,
      head back like that
      with Halley's Comet hair.
Years from now when I hear the news of his death
I'll remember that night and this poem,
Shivering a little as I did then,
Surprising myself
      with the thought of salmon
      shooting up the rapids of his brain,
What he was—near as a grosbeak, far as Orion,
      the sound of mice moving delicately
      in the walls of his flesh.

# The Last Halloween

The last night he was a ghost
Doors opened to his touch
And slipped bits of flesh
Into his pillow case.

Before home he reached down
To feel if he received
What he desired.
He liked kisses best.
They were chewy
And stuck to his teeth.

At home on bed he emptied
Out his dreams and, slipping
The pillow back in its case,
Assembled the flesh
To the last wrinkled breath
Of a rotting man.

He tried on the corpse
To see how it would fit.
And answering the door
That had been knocked
He saw a coffin worn
With earth, a tombstone
Head, and little leaves
For feet.

He was too old
To pretend
To be anything
Else.

# Metaphor

Seeing a boy stare in through the glass,
The adult magazine store where I'm standing,
I know he's aching for pictures of skin
That can make a metaphor of his hand,
Thinking of times his house is suddenly empty
And rushing her familiar flesh from hiding
He can fill his bed with nakedness and dream
She touches him softly as a mirror.
And I think of Hypatia,
Lecturer in philosophy at the Alexandrian Museum,
Who, though loved by many, remained a virgin.
Once, when a student confessed his total love,
She, lifting her dress to her waist, said:
"What you love is this,
And nothing beautiful."
And here stands this boy
Who must close his eyes to see
A girl more real, more naked
Than pictures.

## For Those Who No Longer Go Ahhh . . .

Not watching the fireworks
I thought how much more beautiful
Were the faces illuminated—
Some thinking for the first time
How like orgasm the explosions,
A thought now old to me,
Yet for them how much meaning,
I knew, I remembered.

Out of our lives forever
Hundreds of firework faces.
Where they are going
Is to the sigh and dissolution
After the flashing flower,
After the falling petals,
Silence looking upward
Hoping what's next is more beautiful.

# Last Words

As this girl lay asleep on the beach
An ant crawled up her nose and laid its eggs
And when they hatched and ate into her brain
She clawed away her face and died screaming.
Or that deep-sea diver whose pressurized suit burst
Who was squeezed a liquid pulp of flesh
Up the air hose onto the deck,
A long strand of human spaghetti.
Or that man on a Japanese train killed by the severed leg
Of a suicide who jumped from a passing train,
A hundred miles an hour through his window.
Or Li Po launching himself like a paper boat toward the moon.
Or Aeschylus strolling along the shore
When an eagle, looking for a stone to crack a turtle's shell,
Spotted his pate gleaming in the sun.
Or that Pompeii boy immortalized in lava.
Or the unearthed coffin, the lid scratched and bloody inside.
Or abandoned by his family, the old Eskimo circled by wolves.
Or Superman no longer faster than a speeding bullet through his head.
Or Santa's helicopter crashing in a shopping center of expectant children.
Or six children trampled to death in Cairo by a mob
Rushing to a church where the Virgin had just appeared.
These deaths speak for themselves. They don't need last words.
As for me, I'm not looking into the sky for falling flowerpots.
Yet any second sights of a rifle may fix on my brain.
Fourteen humans walked alive that day a perfect stranger
By the name of Whitman up in a tower of higher learning
Shot them down one by one. Just like that. Dead.
I think of that old man stoned by three children
            who jeered him out of his house.
If someone told me that's how I'd die in fifty years
I wouldn't believe it. Did anyone tell the old man?

How will I die? Cleaning a gun with my eyes?
Walking into a mirror? Driving into a tree to avoid a porcupine,
　　　　my learner's permit in my pocket?
I know the old philosophies. Yes, I've already died in a way.
My boyhood and all that. Showers of fingernails and hair.
The constant sloughing off of the cells of my body.
The death of all the semen that has left me.
My turds, moving to their own bewildered death.
Maybe it'll be like that first night in San Francisco
Waking up to go to the bathroom in Milwaukee,
And getting out of my old bed I walk into a new wall.
Maybe it'll be coming up or going down stairs in the dark
Thinking there's one more step when there isn't
Or not one more step when there is.
Will I choke on a bone, or be swallowed by a whale?
Or a death brimming with allusions—
Tugging a book from the tightly packed shelf
　　　　I pull my whole bookcase over on me.
Or slow death: torture, cancer, leprosy, senility,
Or exotic: voodooed, cannibalized, human-sacrificed,
　　　　devoured by man-eating plant.
Which is worse, being eaten alive or starving to death?
Dying crying for help or begging for mercy?
Yawning as the bomb drops in my mouth,
Sneezing in the avalanche zone,
Done in by hiccups that can't be stopped,
Boarding the *Titanic* assured it's unsinkable,
Or like in Stekel, that man who hid under the outhouse seat
And disemboweled his wife from beneath with a butcher knife.
　　　　I look before sitting.
Or seeing my ultimate vision of absolute beauty
I scream as in horror comics—"AAARRRGGGHHH!!!"
Will I die laughing? Be struck by lightning?
　　　　Will I never know what hit me?

Maybe the sky will fall on me.
Maybe the ground'll just open up under me.
Maybe a gang of boys'll pour gasoline over me and light me.
      Or will it be a case of spontaneous combustion?
Will I be mistaken for a deer during deer season?
Or like Tita Piaz who climbed 9000 feet of sheer rock 300 times
      with his son strapped to his back, only to die in a fall
      down his steps?

And when am I going to die? I'd like to know.
I don't want to get there when the show's half over.
I don't want to fall asleep. I'll have to poke myself.
I don't want to miss my death the way I missed my birth.
I sit here and plan my last words. I'm going to be prepared.
As in murder mysteries where the victim lies dying
And the hero holds him and says—"Who did it?"
In the same way they'll gather round me and ask—
      "What does this poem mean?"
      or "Do you really think *that* is beautiful?"
And then, like the murdered victim, I'll mumble far away
Feverishly trying to think of something profound and rising in pitch
      gasp
"It was It was It was It was . . ."
Then slumping back I die.

What will I say? Shall I make fart sounds with my lips?
Should I tell where the treasure's hidden?
Should I utter *Wanbli Galeshka wana ni he o who e?*
      My bestfriend's name?
Or make make-believe deathrattles better than birdlovers
      warble songs of their favorite birds?
Or should I join the chorus of thousands who shriek "AAAIIIEEE!!!"
      or the thousands who simply go "O"
      or "Ugh" or "Oof" or "Whoops"
Or should I press finger to lips in the sign of silence?
Not content with ruling the world, Nero, wanting to be its

supreme actor and musician, ordered full houses and
awarded himself all the prizes, and while he sang
no one could leave, though many pretended to die
in order to be carried out as corpses. Shall I say
as he did when forced to commit suicide—
"What a great artist the world is losing!"
Or like Rabelais—"Bring down the curtain the farce is finished,"
and later as the priests surrounded him,
he, with a straight face, sighed—
"I go to seek a great perhaps."
Or like the Comtesse de Vercelles, according to Rousseau—
"In the agonies of death she broke wind loudly. 'Good!'
she said, 'A woman who can fart is not yet dead.' "
Or like Saint Boniface as boiling lead was poured down his throat—
"I thank thee Lord Jesus, Son of the Living God!"
Or Saint Lawrence, broiled on a gridiron—"This side is done now,
turn me over."
Or Emily Dickinson—"I must go in, the fog is rising."
Or Beddoes—"I ought to have been among other things
a good poet."
Or Lindsay, full of lysol—"They tried to get me . . .
I got them first."
Or Socrates—"Crito, I owe a cock to Asclepius,
will you remember to pay the debt?"
Or Chopin—"Swear to make them cut me open
so I won't be buried alive."
Or Scriabin, his face engulfed in gangrene—
"Suffering is necessary."
Or Marie Antoinette, having stepped on the executioner's foot—
"I beg your pardon."
Or Huey Long—"I wonder why he shot me?"
Or Millard Fillmore—"The nourishment is palatable."
Or P. T. Barnum—"How were the receipts today
in Madison Square Garden?"
Or Carl Panzarm, slayer of 23 persons—"I wish the whole human race
had one neck and I had my hands around it."

Or Jean Barre, 19, guillotined for mutilating a crucifix—
      "I never thought they'd put a gentleman to death
      for committing such a trifle."
Or da Vinci—"I have offended God and man
      because my work wasn't good enough."
Or Vanzetti—"I am innocent."
Zeno, founder of the Stoic school, striking the ground with one fist—
      "I come, I come, why do you call for me?"
W. Palmer, stepping off the gallows—"Are you sure it's safe?"
Metchnikoff the bacteriologist—"Look in my intestines carefully
      for I think there is something there now."
John Wilkes Booth—"Tell my mother I died for my country."
Dylan Thomas—"I've had 18 straight whiskies. I think that's
      the record."
Dutch Schultz—"French Canadian bean soup!"
Byron—"I want to go to sleep now."
Joyce—"Does nobody understand?"

Must I be the scribe of each word I speak,
      never knowing if it will be my last?
Or should someone else be my full-time scribe
      (in case deathfits keep me from writing them down)
Always ready to put ear to my lips
      in case it should be a whisper?
"Rosebud." "More weight." "More light."
"Now it is come." "Now I die." "So this is death?"
"Thank you." "Farewell!" "Hurrah!" "Boo!"
      "Can this last long?" "It is finished."
Or like H. G. Wells—"I'm alright. Go away."
Or like Sam Goldwyn—"I never thought I'd live to see the day."
Or like John Wolcott when asked if anything could be done for him—
      "Bring back my youth."

I tell myself what my last words will be,
Hoping I don't get stage fright.
Hoping I don't get laryngitis.

13

Hoping someone will hear them.
Hoping I'm not interrupted.
Hoping I don't forget what they are.
From now on everything I say and write
Are my last words.

## Applause

Striking the palms of hands together, quick smart blows,
        producing abrupt sharp sounds,
        expresses their satisfaction.
After the performance, they do this.
It is called clapping. I sit and observe,
        that my actions will not be improper.
Am I allowed to do this? Softly at first, I begin,
        scared the man next to me may growl—
        "Quiet! Don't you know this is for *us* to do?
        Children should be seen not heard. Grow up!"

Am I a grown up? I've made up my mind.
But how should I hold my hands?
Up to my breast, or down by my genitals?
Cupped and weak, or flat and firm?
Elbows flush with my sides, or flaring?
Should one hand be still (which one?) and be slapped by the other?
Or should I take wide strokes with both as if trying to take off,
        or pull invisible taffy?
What's the rhythm, rapid or slow?
Do I pat daintily with nose in the air?
Or hard like pounding a nail in?
I'm not used to hitting myself.

Ladies flowing in minks (little stuffed heads
        with black plastic eyes staring from breasts)
        tap their programs on purses.
They've squinted at them throughout the performance,
        rustling the pages, fanning their faces.
        As they leave they forget them.

How many came to hear the music?
How many secretly hoped the performer would make a mistake
        or forget the piece halfway through?

How many nodded off digesting their dinners,
        or peered sideways searching for someone attractive?
Where are those who disappeared during intermission?

I think of cabbages and tomatoes hurled on stages of yore.
I think of orgious ovations lasting three hours.
Why at the end of a symphony doesn't the audience
        carry the players off on their shoulders
        like fans pouring onto the field after a victory?
Hugo's *Hernani*, on opening night
        the audience burned down the theater
        and tried lynching the actors.
On "Queen for a Day" mothers broke down competing at misery,
        while the applause-o-meter leapt to crown
        the champion of disasters.

Are they afraid not to clap?
They don't need idiot cards.
After the most passionate music they clap loudest.
They know how to break the spell.
Is the sound of their clapping more beautiful than the music?
Why don't they clap through the entire performance?
After all, who's really performing?
What does the virtuoso think when at the last note—cough, cough,
        and then the avalanche of praise?
Does he listen to the textures of thousands of fingers?
Does he go into the audience asking for autographs?
Does he lob rotten eggs at the box seats?
Does he clap for himself?
He's seen the seals at the zoo.
If the audience really appreciates beauty why don't they scream
        for hours, clapping till their hands get so hot they melt off
        and they clap faster and faster with their feet and
        they drop off and they clap their limbs, teeth, gums,
        intestines and genitals till all that's left is a huge arena
        of smoking dismembered bodies?

I'm waiting for the time when no one claps.
Paralyzed in silent epiphany. Hands frozen in prayer.
Who claps for lightning?
Who claps for the bowel movement?
After apocalyptic orgasm who claps?
Who claps at a great man's death?
How many are virtuosos of their lives?
People were applauding when Lincoln was shot.
When Jesus was crucified who applauded?
Who stood and demanded an encore?
What kind of ovation did he get?
Blake saw his brother's soul rise through the ceiling
                to heaven, clapping.
Coffin lids clap only once.
If we must clap, why can't it be in soundless slow-motion
                like a butterfly drying its wings?
I clap with my eyes.
My heart claps with one hand.

When I think of my death do I imagine my favorite symphony
                rising to climax and I, maestro at the finale,
                collapsing with romantic gesture,
                audience filing out silent with heads bowed?
Beethoven at the premiere of his Ninth, stone deaf,
                conducting the last time in his life—
                when it was over, he, being several measures off,
                kept waving his arms during the deafening roar.

Audience and performer are gone now, and I'm still sitting.
Clapping. I've learned how. I'll always clap last
                so I add to the total performance.
My art is small, yet heard after all.
Do you think I stay home nights to practice my clapping?
Or am I designing concert halls with pillories for hands?
Am I just one of the audience who couldn't go home
                without finding what he lost:

a wallet, a scarf, a key, the program
on which I jotted notes for this poem?

Once at a reading I deliberately clapped after a lousy poem.
Soon the whole room was earthquaking claps:
Clap. CLAP.CLAP. CLAP!CLAP!CLAP!
        CLAP!!CLAP!!CLAP!!CLAP!!
Do you think I like applause after this poem or any poem?
Do you think I love the silence after my voice has stopped?
Yet I've heard the refusal of praise is only the wish
        to be praised twice.
Each clap stings like the challenge to a duel.
The clock's hands clap as I grow old.
The typewriter claps as I write this.
Can clapping ever be the same?
After reading this will I hear only breathing?
After writing this will I sit here and clap loud and long?

# Wrong Number

Who is this? Who is this?
        No answer.
Sound of sea from shell.
Long breakers of silence.

Hello? Hello? Is anyone there?
        No answer.
Sound of submarine propellers.
Sound of muffled beehives.

When the phone rings and you answer
        and nothing but silence greets you
And each hello you say louder
        the silence that follows deepens,
And when you yell "Who are you?
        Why don't you say something?"
And the other end says nothing,
        why hang up with a bang
When you can listen to them listening,
        or read them this poem?

Anytime you lift the receiver
You could hear panting or moaning or maniac cackling
Or the low voice—"I'm gonna strangle ya tonight!" Click.
Or—"As you hear me a long needle is shooting from the earpiece
        into your brain!" Click.
Or call after call—"Is Jim there?"
Finally the same voice calls—"This is Jim
        have there been any calls for me?" Click.
Or after guessing the largest state—"That's right!
        You win a thousand soggy cigar butts!" Click.

All the numbers in the phonebook
      are at our fingertips.
Anything we want to say we can say
      and hang up and never be traced.
Hundreds of men phoning hundreds of women at random
      to passionately detail their desires.
How many listen? How many girls make erotic phonecalls?
      I'm still waiting.
Why don't I get calls saying—"I'm young. I'm beautiful.
      I want to know you."
If you're as beautiful as your voice come right over!
How close we must be already,
      our lips at each other's ear.

I've dialed ears with my tongue
      trying to get through to genitals.
I've dialed each voice on the telephones of the body
      for weather predictions, inspirational messages,
      information, the correct time.
I wanted to squeeze through the wires like fireflies!
How often I dashed down rollerskate stairs
      finding no one there but the dial tone.

Mattresses speaking.
Hello, mattresses? Could you please
      connect me with pogo sticks?
Sorry, this is toilet floats
      not artificial larynxes.
No, this is toupees not tepees.
Sorry, this is the morgue
      not birth certificates.

The boy voice hears me say—"Hello?"
"Hello," it says, "is this the insane asylum?"
My breath moistens the mouthpiece—"I'm sorry
      you must have the wrong ..." Click.

Sound of ice against keel.
A record of deathrattles.

I dial 0.
Operator, could you please tell me who I am?
Hello, she says, I have some bad news: your father just died.
Death, I should've known you were never too busy
        to be reached in an emergency
        to scream the soft ambulances of sleep.
When will you call collect long distance person to person
        through transoceanic cables of my flesh, your voice
        breaking through my heart's busy signal?
Death, I'm warning you! Poets listen in on extensions.
They want to make a living tapping you
Saying things like "Maggots connect us to Cosmic Switchboard,"
        or "Embalming robs our graves of telephones,"
        or "The piece of steak on our fork says—
        'Guess who this is?' "
Death, why must you go on and on like this?
My ear's turning into a cauliflower.
Don't you get tired of shooting the breeze?
Must I knock on the wall and say—"I have to let you go
        someone's at the door"
Or smash GOODBYE in your coffin ear?
Later, I'll know your call by the ring of thunder
        and I'll ease a cloud down to hear
        your delicate nuzzlers chew into my listening.

Holding this paper to my ear is the line dead?
Is someone dying, gasping on the floor, my voice
        tingling in their hand?
Is writing this like dialing any number at random to sob I just
        have to talk to one human being to tell my life my
        words tottering tightrope walkers into your ears and
        then after an hour's lost world pretend to be choking—
        *the poison ... it's beginning to work ... can't breathe ...*

click, hello? Hello? and you know the rest of your life
        you could've saved me?
My eyes ring. It's this poem again. It wants more images.

Maybe I'm really only interested in calling myself.
But the line's always busy. Who could be talking so long to me?
A hearse pulls up the drive. They say they've come for my body.
        Some boy must be pulling a prank.
In the nursing home I count the telephone poles
        that fly past my window,
        taking messages I forgot for my mother.
Sound of wind over frozen explorers.
Sound of buzz-sawed trees.
Windows are rattling.
Everything is rattling its receivers.
How can I answer them all?
So old I forget who is calling?
And the pillow listens to a shell
Washed up in someone's dream.
What creature lived in here?
Is this the call I've waited for all my life?
I try to decide should I answer.
I worry it might be the wrong number.
If I lift the receiver I'm afraid
I might say goodbye.

## Tyranny of Images

Pilgrims to Mecca burned out their eyes with hot irons
      saying nothing more beautiful could be seen
      and therefore would see nothing more.
Everywhere I look hot irons brandish to blind me to ecstasy.
      I cannot stop seeing.
I have elephantiasis of beauty, must carry my eyes in a wheelbarrow.

Images besiege me. Images enslave me.
They erect me in front of beauty firing squads
      and pump me with epiphany bullets.
They stick fingers down my throat so I vomit and eat more.
They force me to say what I don't want to say.
      I try to say love, turd comes out.
      I try to say turd, God comes out.
They dangle me from nooses of insight and wonder.
They draw and quarter me with fascination.
There is no armor against this onslaught.
I leak. Images gush in. There are never enough
      watertight compartments.

In the vast whirlpool each object sucks the poet
      who struggles to surface speaking in bubbles.
Volvox! Gnomon! Baleen! Uvula! Aureole! Catkins! Stomata!
      each worthy of millions of poems!
Rosin! Gristle! Synapse! Boomerang! Orangutan! Dishrags! Watchfobs!
      Ultra-Rilkean Double-dildoes!
Someday whole libraries of poems on licking nipples!
Someday poets who only write about potatoes,
      or only about arroyos or fumaroles or rhododendrons,
Or katydids or caryatids or kangaroo pouches or bellybuttons!
Someday oceans of poems on oceans!
Someday mountains of poems on mountains!

And more poems on pinheads than angels!
More poems on snowflakes than I can ever read,
    no two identical!
Paeans on perineums! Epics on epiglottis!
Eclogues on undulating fields of villi!
Sagas on sequoias and mayflies!
Concordances of xylem and phloem!
Each leaf that falls shall have its elegy!
Each grain of sand its laureate!
What hundred things should I liken lichen to?
Objects in this room (more here to write
    than hundred lifetimes)
Hurtle themselves at me!
Like bats in my hair! Like mosquitos at bedtime!
Moths, dazzled, thinking me a candle!
Lemmings marching onto me thinking I'm the sea!

Images wriggle on hooks to see which one will fry me in its poem.
They stick guns in my ribs and say—"Reach for the sky!"
My ears are deeper than holes in space.
My nose smells Thanksgiving on other planets.
My eyes are the most powerful telescopes and microscopes.
Girls don't realize I'm their vagina and their gentle finger.
Boys don't realize I'm their cock and fist slippery with their own saliva.
All the turds in the world past and present, believing me Sewer God,
    they creep toward me.
How can I help but dive on the grenade embracing the joyous
    hot leaves of shrapnel?
I'm embedded in euphoric lava.
I unleash my brain and let it wander from my body
    and when it returns it sniffs and urinates
    golden on my imagination.
I'm huddled in a tent, starving, freezing,
    trying to be the first to the pole,
    as glaciers I wrote years ago ponder by,
    scribbling the last entry in the diary of my flesh.
My mind's an orgy in a hall of mirrors.

How can anyone not be poet?
How can anyone say everything's been said,
          or there's nothing to write about?
Each place, object, creature, experience, relationship
          is waiting for poets
          to plant their flags on its continent.
Quetico! Geode! Jack-in-the-Pulpit!
Muskelunge! Dragonfly! Ruby-crowned Kinglet!
Rivulet! Goosebumps! Vernix! Syzygy!
Coprolite! Ichnolite! Fulgurite! Foghorn!
Equinox! Alpenglow! Embryos! Rainbows!
Blowjobs! Why has no poet devoted himself to you?
If I were to write only of you how much I could say!
And to think no poet has found it impossible
          to write anything but odes to Fucking!
What Poetry could say about Orgasm
          would take more than all Bibles together!
O why am I not continually writing poems
          being so awed and sensitive to consciousness of life?
Why isn't everyone writing fast as they can
          a pen in each hand, foot, mouth, and anus
          scribbling simultaneous?
Why aren't there blizzards of poems?
The earth deluged with poems rising like white skyscrapers overhead!
No time to go back and read what I write or anyone's written!
Impossible to read in a hundred years all that's writ in a minute!
          Bees enveloping the beekeeper.
Worlds pouring from the gumball machine till the Earth disappears.
This poem does not want to end.
It expects me to keep writing till I drop dead
And another must take the pen from my hand
          and keep on going where I left off
          till they drop dead
And another must take up the pen,
          on and on.

**25**

The millions of poems within me more beautiful than I'll ever write
    are ready.
They know who can't close his eyes without hearing
    opening cocoons.
They know who wears rearview mirrors on his head as he writes
    to catch images sneaking up on him.
They know who is surrounded by so many poems
    it will take a whole life to find his way out.

The clouds go by. Do I need to say what they look like?
    Do I need to say anything?
I dream the clouds are poems I wrote when I was God,
    paper from which the words could only fall.
I've become too many things. It's easy, too easy.
Now I begin to feel poets should wait, wait
    when images subtly tumesce their minds,
    not touch themselves,
Till five minutes before death, and then
    as simple and direct as possible
    scrawl their one and only poem.
I cannot do this. I was born too soon.
But there are temporary exits from this stage
    and I know an image can be my trapdoor:
I perform the Indian Rope Trick on myself.
My phallus rises. I climb its sensual rungs and disappear
    amid the thunder and the clouds.

## Lost Sheep

Trying to fall asleep
        an idea for a poem
            kept me awake.
Too tired to jot it down
        I put myself to sleep
            repeating it.
In the morning I woke
        remembering I'd remember
            what I forgot.

# Toward the Definition of a Tree
## While a Cold Orange Is Rolled on My Forehead

If I were to show you two hands
        joined by a wrist—
One hand reaching into sky,
One hand reaching into earth,
        both stretching like a tug of war
        when neither side budges,
Would you say—"What a way to pray!"
Or "When'll they learn to shake hands?"
Or "That's not what I see.
        I see fireworks shooting
        out either end of a baton."

And if you were to show me twins
        joined at the feet
        smirking—"So there!"
Would I say—"How can they walk
        unless as one walks on his feet
        the other walks on his hands?"
Or "Stand on your hands on a mirror
        and look how your reflection
        holds you up like an acrobat."
Or "All you're saying is
        how much of the iceberg
        we can't see."

# Beyond the Call of Duty

At the general swim
the campers stood silent
staring into the pool.
"A turd!" I yelled.
"Some camper laid a turd
during last night's swim!
No one's going in
till *that* comes out.
Who's going in to get it?"

Sound of showers dripping.
Blue jays in the white pines.
The boys looked down and shivered.

Putting my megaphone down
I volunteered, chest out,
poised from the lifeguard chair.
"Watch me!"
Into turquoise I swanned
beneath muted cheers,
bubbles trailing my cheeks
as I swam
toward the brown thing
on the bottom.
Then clutching the long rigid lump
and rising
I splashed all smiles into air
and opening my mouth
took a big chaw
on the candy bar
I threw there
that morning.

# The Smell That Leads the Nose Tingling Back

Walking through Camp one night
I discovered on the familiar path
        a fresh turd.
Among leaves and moonlight
        the sleek dropping lay,
wisps of steam wavering in the cool.

Remembering the campfire hush
when shadows, sparks, smoke
and dying coals made horror come alive,
        I wondered how one boy
after all the rest were sleeping
dared sneak through pines
        and screams of twigs
to squat and tremble,
        the solid flame
melting loose and slipping free,
the grunted sigh and shiver.

In the morning everyone saw it.
Walking to breakfast I heard them joking,
        accusing each other,
and wondered which boy who laughed
was the one who rose from that place
and ran back through the woods to sleep,
ran back alone under stars.

# The Bewilderment of Laughter

A boy and girl walk past you laughing,
And because they're laughing and you're not,
And because you don't know why they're laughing,
        it's as if they're laughing at you,
Even if they're not,
Even if they're laughing so hard
        they don't even notice you as they pass,
And so walking alone becomes walking lonely,
For no matter how many friends you have
A boy and girl will walk past you laughing
        sometime when you're alone,
And because what's loneliest in you will hear them,
The sound of their laughter will haunt you
        long after they're gone.

So when old men slip and laugh as they fall
        you ask them to be your teachers,
To teach you where Christ laughs in the gospels—
A laugh that makes others laugh,
        a funny laugh, a contagious laugh,
A laugh impossible to hold back,
        a wild laugh, a consoling laugh,
A laugh more profound than prayer or parable,
        a believable laugh,
A laugh that unfolds like a head of lettuce,
        a fresh green laugh,
A laugh that makes heaven without laughing unthinkable,
A laugh that curls lips back not to bare fangs to scare rivals,
A laugh that spreads in ripples till it's lapping round the world,
A laugh only had it been recorded
        slaughter would never have the word laughter in it
        and no one would ever abominate
        the merriment of worms.

But nowhere in scripture does it say "Christ laughed."
Nowhere does he split a gut!
Nowhere does he summersault and cartwheel hooray!
Nowhere does he hug himself laughing himself hoarse!
Nowhere does he jump-up-and-down-laugh-his-ass-off-whoopee!
Nowhere does he spend 40 days and nights in omnipotent conniptions!
Nowhere does he give immortality to fun or the bliss of glee
          or teach a Lord's Prayer full of wisecracks!
And where is he giddy or silly?
And where is he drunken with laughter?
And where does he fracture his funnybone?
And where does he wear jester shoes with curled toes and little bells?
O point out the chapter and verse of his slapstick slaphappy laughter!
Where does he tell how the man without a jaw laughs?
Where does he say the reason we bury corpses
          is so they don't get funny?
Why didn't he make making fart sounds under armpits his disciples?
Why isn't giggling while hiding playing hide'n'seek in the twilight
          a beatitude?
Why isn't baptism epilepsies of laughter?
Wouldn't everything be different if just once the Son of God
          had bent over and cracked a smile?
Was Christ only pulling our leg about eternal damnation?
          (Heaven really only for atheists and heathens?)
When the nails were pounded in
          did no one see the twinkle in his eye?
Did no one but me hear the jokes he told from the cross?
Don't you think he got a kick out of sticking his finger
          through the holes in his hands?
Don't you think he ever chuckled to himself
          as he walked alone?

Our way of laughing grows older as we do:
For some of us it dies before our funeral—

Suddenly we hear ourselves laughing
        like someone who will never be an actor,
And we realize years ago we didn't like people
        who laughed like that.
So we listen to recordings never made
        of laughter bubbling from our mouths
        five, ten, fifteen, twenty, twenty-five birthdays old,
Remembering uncontrollable laughter possessing us
        till it hurt so much we laughed even harder,
        wetting our pants from laughing so hard,
        laughing until we cried. . . .
And so we start repeating the word death over and over,
Death with the word eat in it that will eat us,
Death that's not sorry we tamed our laugh
        so we can turn it on and off like a lightswitch,
Death that sheds no tears we busted our laughingfit buckingbronco,
Death that does not care if we think death is no laughing matter,
Death that does not say death is the punchline,
Death that does not say death has the last laugh,
Death that's never been Christ's flunky or yes-man,
Death that doesn't give a damn if Christ died laughing or cursing,
Death that doesn't consider Christ getting a boner on the cross a blasphemy,
Death that doesn't have to swear on a stack of Bibles
        to tell the Truth,
Death that doesn't give a hoot if we believe no matter how we live
        if we can make God laugh we are saved,
Death we want to believe will touch us like our mother,
        like the mother who consoles her child
        when other children point and laugh,
Death with its skull that never stops grinning
        the grin that never stops touching
        our face from the inside,
And babies may cry when they're born
        but their skulls have been grinning long before
        and don't need a university to learn how,

And how a blind man feels when everyone's laughing
        and he can't see what's so funny,
And how this all brings us back to the boy and the girl,
How they walk toward us and past us laughing
        or from behind us and past us laughing
And walking lonely not laughing we wish we could join them,
        wish we could fill our mouths with those jubilees.


## II


All I've done is fill my mouth with words.
I've composed haikus to monkeyshines and odes to shenanigans.
I've authored the epic of tee-heeing on tip-toe.
I've dissertationed the definitive text of ticklishness.
I've sent humoresque smokesignals from the ancient peaks.
I am the scholar of winks and the archeologist of guffaws.
I've traced the word for laugh in every language back to the sun.
The giggling of Neanderthal children in caves during the sacred ritual
        still reaches my ears.
I hear laughter of rolling down hills and leaping off sand dunes.
I hear laughter of fathers running with sons
        laughing piggyback on their shoulders.
I hear laughter of mothers holding daughters by hands
        and going in a circle so fast
        the little girls fly around in the air.
Yet where is the deep spontaneous laugh I haven't laughed in years?
        My primal laugh, my inexhaustible laugh?
        The laugh in which all of me laughs, not just my mouth?
O how many fatted calves would I kill
        if my laugh that was lost was found?
Will I never again feel the thrill
        breaking up in church so the whole pew shakes
        with wrestled-back gags of laughter?
Will all the times I imitated laughter of morons and opera singers
        never return the way it made all my friends laugh?

And the laughter of my sixth grade class
            when the teacher didn't see my raised hand
            and I ran up to tell her I felt sick
            and before I could say a word
            vomited on her dress
            to become laughingstock of the school for weeks,
Can't I look back on it now and laugh?
I feel like a stone face that's frowned for 5000 years!
Must I wait for all the faces I made in the mirror to become my face
            before delighting in a single cackle?

If there is one laugh worth all the laughs you have left,
            take it now,
And after that thigh-slapping, floor-rolling binge
You won't have to ask—"How long have deformities and deathcamps
            been God's court jester?"
You'll know why children draw the sun with a smiling face.
You'll understand how maniacs can laugh for hours.
You'll know what lies behind the laughter of peekaboo
            and ring-around-the-rosy,
And the laughter of girls in junior high showerrooms,
And the laughter of boys pretending to get dirty jokes,
And the toothless laughter of nursing homes,
The laugh of those finding out they have one month to live,
The laugh of the waterskier rising in bubbles
            as he rises to surface into the returning propeller,
The laugh of dolls you pull the string from their backs and they laugh,
The laugh of the rapist or strangler who has cornered his victim,
The laughter of men who make a living poisoning the earth
            and don't feel guilty,
The laughter of crowds at public tortures and executions,
            the laughter of the guillotined head,
And the hermit who hasn't seen a human in thirty years
            listening to the echo of his laugh across the valley,
And the laughter of siamese twins joined at the mouth,

**35**

The laughter of the man the Sioux buried up to his head
        smeared with honey near an anthill,
Laughter of ants, laughter of anteaters,
Laughter of monkeys and laughing hyenas,
Laughter of aspen and weeping willow,
Laughter of lizards and lampreys and clams,
Laughter of whales and amoebas,
Laughter of volcanoes and earthquakes,
Laughter of exploding stars,
Laughter of earthlings ogling Earth from the moon,
Laughter of the crescent moon's smile,
Laughter of other planets,
The laugh of those who scorn poetry,
The laugh of those deaf since birth,
Obnoxious laugh of those who laugh too loud and long,
Nervous laugh of the inexperienced teacher,
Derisive laugh of the perverted embalmer,
And those who laugh in the face of death,
And those who laugh bad breath in your face,
And those who laugh at their own bad jokes,
And those who laugh behind laughing masks,
And those who laugh through their nose,
And those who laugh while they cry inside,
And those who dimple at the dimpling of buttocks,
And those who double up at the bullfrog's croak,
And those whose job is turning people into pretzels of laughter,
And the man in stitches who splits into stitches—
All the gales of laughter, all the tons of laughs,
        all the laughs in the world
        you will understand.
For as long as you stand under the waterfall of all the laughs of
        your life in an instant
How can you be sad? How can you be lonely knowing a trillion years
        is only a second in Eternity?
And looking through a telescope large as our galaxy
        with an eye big as the sun

Why be unhappy because you can see no more of Infinity
        than an infinitesimal crumb?

Someday you could find yourself when the bird sings in the forest
Listening like the bird to its own overflowing song,
About to discover you can sing without words
        or the lilt of some tune,
That tossing your head back it would rise
        and you'd let it, your laugh,
The way you laughed as a child, your tears,
        the way they loved coming from joy,
Your laughter, your tears, together—
        HO spelled backwards OH,
        HA spelled backwards AH—
And the bird listening as you are
        to both of your songs.

# Falling Through

On his back, hands behind head,
the cloud gazes down at me
wondering what I look like.
He breathes deep, yawns,
stretches against the sky,
and feeling the warm wind surround him
like dreams, he wishes
he could lie against the sky forever.
*It looks like ... that could be legs,*
*those could be arms, and that might be a head ...*
*It looks like a boy, a man, a cloud?*
But the cloud tires of searching for words.
He'd rather just lie in the sun
listening to himself breathe.

As the sun sets, the cloud turns colors,
shivers, blows a sprig of lightning
from between his teeth.
He looks down at me and knows
I'm a mist of flesh on dust.
*Soon,* he thinks, *it will be drizzling,*
*and there will be soft thunder.*
Dozing off, the cloud sighs:
*It looks like ... a pillow ... a bed?*
*I wonder if I could lie down on that body*
*without falling through, and sleep*
*as it drifted across the earth.*

By night the sky was cloudless,
and the field was quiet with fog.

# FACTORY

# Factory

The machines waited for me.
Waited for me to be born and grow young,
For the totempoles of my personality to be carved,
　　　and the slow pyramid of days
To rise around me, to be robbed and forgotten,
They waited where I would come to be,
　　　a point on earth,
The green machines of the factory,
　　　the noise of the miraculous machines of the factory,
Waited for me to laugh so many times,
　　　to fall asleep and rise awake so many times,
　　　to see as a child all the people I did not want to be,
And for suicide to long for me as the years ran into the mirror
　　　disguising itself as I grew old
　　　in eyes that grew old
As multitudes worked on machines I would work on,
　　　worked, ceased to exist, and died,
For me they waited, patiently, the machines,
　　　all the time in the world,
As requiems waited for my ears
　　　they waited,
As naked magazines waited for my eyes
　　　they waited,
As I waited for soft machines like mine
　　　time zones away from me, unknown to me,
　　　face, flesh, all the ways of saying goodbye,
While all my possibilities, like hand over hand on a bat
　　　to see who bats first, end up choking the air—
While all my lives leap into lifeboats

shrieking—"You can't afford to kill time
while time is killing you!"
Before I said *Only the religion whose command before all others
is Thou Shalt Not Work shall I hosanna,*
Before I said *Not only underground are the minds of men
eaten by maggots,*
Before I said *I would rather be dead
than sweat at the work of zombies,*
The machines waited.


Now the factory imagines I am there,
The clock keeps watching me while it works
        to see how much time it has left.
How much does it get paid? Are coffins the safes
        where it keeps its cash?
I see my shadow working on the shadow of a machine.
Everywhere I look I am surrounded by giant machines—
Machines that breathe me till I become stale
        and new windows of meat must be opened.
Each year of my name they ran, day and night,
Each time I kissed, each time I learned a new word,
        or name of a color, or how to spell boy,
Night, day, without stopping, in the same place running,
Running as I learned how to walk, talk, read, count, tell time
        and every time I ever ran alone
        pretending to be a wild black stallion,
They ran as I thought never (my eyes in the clouds)
        would my future corpse need to be buried
        premature in slavery of exchange to contemplate
        the leisure vacations of photosynthesis and limnology
        and the retirement of tombstone inscriptions
        into veils that veronica the earth,
They ran, and I never heard them,
        never stopped to hear them coming,
All the times walking to school and back,
All the times playing sick to stay home and have fun,

All the summers of my summer vacations
I never once thought I'd live to sacrifice my dwindling fleshbloom
        packaging the finishing touches on America's decay
For money to earn me so I can write in the future
        about what I am now, then am no longer,
Shortening the lifespan of planet for 6¢ a minute
        so I can elegize the lifespan of beauty and my life,
So I can say before my parents ever met
        machines were blaring the same hysterical noise,
So I can say they were waiting for me
        every mouthful of food I swallowed,
So I can say they were waiting for me
        every time paper eyes of paper nakedness
        watched my hands perform the ritual of dreams,
So I can say each second so many die so many are born,
        like rapid snapping of fingers, snap, snap,
        snap you live, snap you die, snap you live and die again!
Each day of my life *is my life*!

So, winding my watch before work
        with the galaxies of my fingerprints—
        each twist of my lifeline a dungeon of ticks—
I wondered was it for this
        my hide'n'seek Huckleberryhood?
And pondered how each day goes to its grave single file
        without the corpse of what I might have been,
Yet the hour hand is so slow
        no one will ever see it move.

Each of the great works never written
By those who work in factories so they can write words,
        what they say will be great words,
Does not care, does not wait to be written—
At the end of a day's work he who left his mind
        eight hours at his writing desk for the repugnance
        of metal on metal, noise on noise,

**43**

Sits down with his pen as if he had already written
        the great words of his dreams.
His feet feel like nursing homes for wheelchairs,
His ears an inferno of crickets,
And he says—"I feel like the grave of someone I loved"
And dreams of being hired to hammock-drowse
        outside where workers work
        to contemplate the utopias of sleep
Or to conduct tours of the plant reciting by heart
        the godliest glossolalias of divine frenzy.
Each day, those reaching the cliff of their last words
        waterfall into the gorges of night, wondering
*How much do corpses get paid for working underground?*
*How much should they receive for urging their eyes to become*
        *the eyes on butterfly wings, peacock tails, and potatoes?*
*How much to package their innards into the innards of trees*
        *and leaves that creep down shirtfronts of children*
        *hiding in them?*
*How much to coax their hearts into the eight hearts*
        *of the hermaphroditic nightcrawler or into the pink stars*
        *that are the noses of moles?*
*What union do corpses join? How do they feel, more segregated*
        *than old people, when we keep them from humans that live—*
        as if their bodies weren't the bodies we loved
        and called by the names we loved them by—
        *and cut the dandelions from their faces?*


Perhaps I have never left the factory.
Perhaps I'm made to dream the 16 hours my identity flees.
It's the drug in the water that does it, remarkable.
To think I'll work here forever thinking I go home and return
        and do all sorts of things in between,
        like writing this poem—
Of course I'm not writing this poem!
I'm on the machine now packaging endless ends of aluminum
        for the tops and bottoms of cans.

Our foreman laughed—"You'll wake up in the middle of the night
        as if you're working. It's so easy
        you can do it in your sleep."
And I know that in one day owning this place
I'd make more than if my life worked my lifetime here.
In my lifetime I'd make more than all the workers combined.
Then I could envy those who make a million a second—
To them the prostitutes must be most beautiful
        and pornography religion that is never disbelieved.
To those, this memo, dashed during breaks in slavery
        whose chains regenerate faster than tails of salamanders
        or penis's reengorgement.
To my soul wondering if I have a body or not: Huck, Huck,
        look down at your funeral from lofts of the barn o' blue,
Look down at me dreaming my deathbed in factory,
        machines gone berserk, drowning in a sea of lids,
Dying where no one could hear my last whisper
        for industries of scholars to unhieroglyph—
Where the noise is so loud that if I screamed louder than I can
        no one would hear me, not even myself,
Where the bathroom stalls are scratched with the multiplication
        of men's lives in money, the most begging graffiti,
Where it is not I who wrote this tomb, but a machine,
        and the earplugs, and the timeclock
Waiting so many times to pick up the card that tells me my name,
Where metal cries louder than human yearning to return
        underearth,
And the first shift can't wait to go home,
And the second shift can't wait to go home,
And the third shift can't wait for the millions
        of alarmclocks to begin ringing
As I struggle with iron in my face,
Hooked fish played back and forth to work
        by unseen fisherman on unseen shore,
Day after day my intestines unwinding around me
Until I am a mountain of waste

From whose depths all that is left of me,
        a penis and a mouth,
Dreams of reaching the peak of all I contained,
Dreams of jerking that fisherman from the earth
        and dragging him to the pearls
        in the jaws of the giant clams of the sky. . . .

## II

"All you have to do is stand here
        and package lids as they come from the press
        checking for defects every so often.
Shove enough lids in the bag like this,
Stand the filled bag on end like this,
Fold over the top like this,
Pull enough tape off
        and tape it like this,
Then stack 'em like this on the skid."

How many watching me watch the woman
        teach me my job
Remembered *their* first day on the job,
Remembered wondering what the woman felt
        teaching them in a minute
        the work she'd done all her life,
Showing them so fast all they needed to know?
How many could still remember who they were in search of a living—
Name, address, telephone, age, sex, race,
Single, married, children, parents, what they do or why they died,
Health record, police record, military record, social security #,
        how far in school, everywhere worked, why quit or fired,
        everything written here is true, signature, interview,
        the long wait, the call "you're hired"—
Could still see themselves led through the factory
        to the spot they would work on,
        strange then and now so familiar?

This is the hall big as a football field.
Here are the 24 presses chewing can lids
        from hand-fed sheets of aluminum.
Here are the 10 minsters chomping poptops
        nonstop into lids scooped into their jaws.
Machines large as locomotives,
        louder than loudest rockgroup explosions,
Screeching so loud you go deaf without earplugs,
        where the only way to speak is to gesture,
Or bending to your ear as if I were telling a secret
        the yell from my cupped hands less than a whisper.


Now the film of myself each day on the job begins.
I see myself enter the factory, led to the spot I will work on.
I see myself adjusting the earplugs to stopper the deluge of sound.
I see the woman who showed me the job
        she'd done her whole life in a minute
Let me take over, and the minute she left how I fumbled,
        how the lids gushed all over the floor
And when the foreman rushed over and I hollered—
        "Something's wrong! It's too fast!
        No one can work at this speed!"
How he stared and the stares of the others
        who couldn't hear what I said but could tell.
And I gulped, This "Beat the Clock" stunt
        must be performed *eight hours*
        before the lunatic buzzer itself
        becomes consolation prize.


Yet sooner than I thought, I mastered the rhythms,
        turned myself into a flywheel dervish,
And can't deny being thrilled by the breakthrough
        from clumsy to graceful—

**47**

Though old-timers scowled as if it took years
        to learn all the fine points.
But long after my pride in doing such a good job
        turned into days crossed off the calendar
        each night before pulling out the alarm
            I woke to push in,
            up, eat, go, work, eat, work, back, eat, sleep,
All the days I would work stared
        ahead of me the line of machines,
        behind me the line of machines,
Each with a worker working as I work,
        doing the same job that I do,
Working within sight of the wall clock
        whose second hand is still moving.

### III

Thus as the foreman watched me from the corner of his eye
        as I watched him from the corner of mine
        pretending to be doing my best
            as if I didn't know I was under inspection,
I relished the words I would write
        intoned in this factory where no one could hear them,
        swallowed in the shrill-greased ecstasy of machines
            as I led processions of naked acolytes
        sopranoing Athenian epitaphs, candles in their hands.

To write this poem, to bring the word beautiful into Factory
You must never forget when the lids first come from the press
        they are hot, they are almost slippery.
You must never forget since each tube holds 350 lids
        and each crate holds 20 tubes and each day I fill 40 crates
From my work alone 280,000 lids each day—
        huge aluminum worm wriggling one mile long
        into the cadaver of America.

You must never forget 14 million cans each day
        from a single factory!
5,110,000,000 cans each year from a single factory!
More throwaway cans each year than human beings on this planet!
Every high, every heartbeat of your life
        the machines have been running.
Every time you heard a pianissimo
        the earsplitting machines have been running.
You've already spent more time working here
        than making love,
More time working here than lying on hills
        looking at the sky.
Each of your favorite books you must pilgrimage here to age,
        to absorb and exude wisdom,
To think of those who worked here before you
        and those who will work here after you.
You must say to yourself—"If I don't work here
        this poem won't be able to write me."
And asked—"What's that smell?" you must remember
        on your clothes, on your skin, in your lungs
        and when the breeze is just right through your bedroom window
        the smell of the factory.
You must brainstorm machines and workers are like poets and readers:
        the poets eat sheets of steel and press them into words
        that are the ends of containers,
The reader stands in one place shifting from foot to foot,
        crating and crating,
Searching for defects so the noisemaker can be shut down
        and while white-coated mechanics scurry to fix it
        like doctors around a sick president, he can take a break,
        get a drink, take a crap, unwrap some butterscotch to suck on,
        glimpse a glimpse of second-shift sunset,
        watch the guard lower the flag.

To birth this womb, to do for Continental Can Company
        what Walt Whitman did for America,

You must celebrate machine-shop rendezvous!
You must loafe observing a disc of aluminum!
You must sing the security of treadmills
        remembering where you are today
            you were yesterday
            you will be tomorrow.
So, after suicide invites you through the naked mirror
        and poetry dares you to dive headfirst into the sky,
After memorizing the discovery of fire, tools, speech,
        agriculture, industry,
And all the inventors, inventions and dates
        of the last 10,000 years you got a 100 on in History,
And after the ceaseless history of human war
        reads the eyes in your face,
Faced with the obituary of man,
Caught in the deathrattle of the world,
        from the deathblows of pollution,
        from the deathknells of overpopulation,
        from factories which are the deathbeds of Nature
            and the seedbeds of bombs,
After contemplating the graveyard of elegies,
        the immortality of maggots
        and the immolation of the sun,
Then, Antler, or whatever your name is,
Enjoy returning prodigal to your machine
        to forget the view from the skyscrapers of money,
        to forget the hosts of human starvations
            belly-bloated or brainwashed in Mammon,
        to forget the sign over the entrance to Auschwitz
            WORK MAKES MAN FREE,
        to forget that working here you accomplice
            the murder of Earth,
        to forget the birds that sing eight hours a day
            daydreaming the salaries of worms,
        to forget how old you must be

to be rich and young before you die,
to forget your mother waking you
from this nightmare
is only a dream—
So nothing called life can torment you with undertakings
and your only responsibility toward mankind
is to check for defects in the ends of cans.

## IV

All I have to do is stand here
and do the same thing all day.
But the job requiring five steps repeated over and over
eight hours every day
is not monotonous.
Only the body and mind finding such work monotonous
is monotonous.
Those who gripe work is boring
gripe they are boring.

Yet if I work hours and the clock says
only five minutes has gone by,
If the last hour working seems longer
than the seven before it,
Won't my last day on the job seem longer
than all the months that preceded it?
Could I have been here more in one day
than someone who's put in ten years?
Or has he learned how to punch in and out
fast as a punching bag?
Don't we both know the way
to the prong of our alarm in the dark?
How long could I work without looking up at the clock?
How long before I was watching its hands
more than watching my own package lids?

It's not so terrible that every second dies
        or that whatever I am every second dies
        or that what we call death
            is death only of the final second,
But it is terrible (not like movies that lead us
        down corridors to doors springing slimy buffooneries)—
Terrible as having to eat meat killed in factories is terrible,
        as having to wear clothes made in factories is terrible,
        as having to live in homes built by strangers
            and exist among millions of strangers
        and be born and buried by strangers is terrible,
Too terrible for terrible to have any meaning—
        that every second dies
            *whoever I could possibly be.*

                    V

Standing in one place all day,
Howl of machines too loud for anything but solitude,
Rhythm of work-movements long ago involuntary as breathing,
As seconds become minutes become hours become days
            become weeks become months
What goes through your brain?
What carries you away?
What soars?

Whatever thought me while I slaved, remember me now!
Conceive me again! Inspire! Absorb! Engross me again!
Come, power of this very spot—
            overwhelm me again!
Fast-motion film of evolution
            on this spot where I work—
Start from the start and leave nothing out!
        Provoke me as you provoked me then!
        Confront me as you confronted me then!

Begin to consider me, everything that happened,
             is happening, will happen on this specific intersection
                  of latitude and longitude!
             I dare you to run wild in me again!
Show me every ocean, mountain, forest, glacier
                  that once actually was where the machine is now!
Show me the pageant of every creature
             born or died on this point on earth,
             that sexed here or ate here or played here
                  or slept here for here was its home!
Show me this factory grown old, abandoned in ruins!
Show me what stands where it stood
             every sunrise the next billion years!
Let me piece together civilizations that don't yet exist
             from their imagined remains!
How long before who's exactly beneath me on the other side of globe
             tires of thinking me?
How long before what every living thing's doing as I work
             no longer fascinates me?
Everywhere I could be and everything I could be doing right now—
             Stagger me with instantaneous travelogues!
Seductive documentaries of every point on earth—
             Tantalize me again!
O Reveille my Reveries to Revelry again!


Which volume from the limitless libraries of my imagination
             should I curl up with first?
The Complete Poetry of Australopithecus?
The Complete Poetry of the Shelley of 3000?
My autobiography before birth? My autobiography after death?
Maybe you'd like to bury your nose in "Puberty of Smell"?
Would you rather browse through "Charon's Coin Collection"
             or "Learning to Breathe"?
Would you rather check out "Putting Mountains Inside Me"
             or "Turning Myself Into Earth"?

Or why not let the wind turn to the page that begins—
        "Even the most ethereal vision of the mystic
            is knowledge much as an amoeba
            might be said to know a man."
Or why not the snapshot album of the faces
        of everyone committing suicide this second?


Every second I work millionaires younger than me
        are fulfilling my wildest desires.
Do other workers love their genitals
        as much as I love mine?
The middle-aged women know how much sex
        the young guys need to think and have.
Old-timers pin nudes above their last stand,
        play tag with lids whizzed at each other,
        the foreman pretends not to notice.
Wistful penises, wistful vaginas
        hark back to their boyhoods and girlhoods
        growing up oblivious to lifetime in factory.
Ah, daydreams of fucking! It's true
        after six hours you've exhausted the repertoire
            but there's nothing like having a boner
        when there's no way to touch it and it won't go away,
And clearer than ever before the old man I become
        pictures my puberty passion—
Just how my penis began making love to me,
        how girls' nipples swooned for my mouth,
How the mirror put its lips against mine
        and kissed me deep with its boyish tongue!


How many boys are assembling plastic models of dinosaurs
        in Wauwatosa this second?
How many boys are pretending their hands are dogfighting biplanes
        in Wauwatosa this second?
How many boys are riding bikes with feet on the handlebars singing
        in Wauwatosa this second?

How many boys are playing "Engulfed Cathedral" on the piano
         in Wauwatosa this second?
How many boys are reading *Martin Eden* in Wauwatosa
         falling in love with poetry this second?
How many boys are jacking off in the Universe this second?

What good does it do to say one second
         is to a human lifetime what a human lifetime
         is to the age of the Milky Way?
What good does it do to say there are as many galaxies
         in the visible universe
         as stars in the Milky Way?
What good does it do to say each of us is a planet
         or that there are millions of planets
         with life in outerspace?

The workers look forward to lunch
         or fucking when they get home.
Long nights of TV look forward to them.
Weekends of movies and bars look forward to them.
Cheering in football stadiums and buying things in stores
         and 50 weeks imagining a 2-week vacation,
         ' all are waiting for them.
Does the baby inside the pregnant woman working ahead of me
         dream of a knock on the door and a check for a million?
When she smokes by the vending machine on her break
         and it's not as if she's staring off into space
         but as if space were staring far off into her eyes,
         can the unborn tell the dead from the living?
Are its ears already dumbfounded by stupor?
Does it already treasure Te Deums of tedium?
What good does it do to say each of us is a universe
         when we're bored with immortality already?

Poetry keeps telling me I'm an obstetrician on 24 hour call
         to deliver the voice of God from my mouth.

Beethoven had a chamberpot installed in his piano stool—
        there wasn't time to leave the keys.
I can't hear the Moonlight without seeing him write it,
        his britches around his ankles.
How long would it take to hear all he wrote
        if I listened eight hours a day?
How long must I dream of squeezing as fast and thick and warm
        for hysters to truck away for consumers to guzzle
        the hops of my nostalgia?
How much do beetles deserve for rolling dung into balls
        to cradle and suckle their young?
Do ants carrying away my lips get overtime?
What kind of raise do corpses get?
What kind of promotion?
How long before the canteen of melodies you can hum
        runs dry?
Or all the poems learned by heart as you toiled,
        typed on small cards—"Poets to Come,"
        "The World Is Too Much With Us," "Man With the Hoe,"
        "Ozymandias," "Mezzo Cammin," "Divina Commedia #1,"
        "There Was a Boy," "In Paths Untrodden," "Gic to Har,"
        "Ode to West Wind, Melancholy, Grecian Urn, Nightingale,"
        "Shine, Perishing Republic," "Futility," "The Broken Oar,"
        "Hay for the Horses," "A Blessing," "To a Stranger,"
        "Strange Meeting," "The Waking," "In a Dark Time,"
        "The End, The Beginning," "Vulture,"
        "Lines Writ by One in the Tower
            Being Young and Condemned to Die" . . .
How long before they get sick of chanting you aloud?

One June afternoon on my break
I walked to the plant entrance and found
A storm, incredible rain, lightning and thunder,
        sky suddenly so dark the street lights came on,
And noticed, on the ground by the open door,

Hundreds of cigaret butts left by those
        who stood, at some time, on the same spot,
Facing the guardhouse, the parking lot, the lawn after that
        to the street, the other factories this side and across,
        the busy freeway beyond,
And realized no one working could hear the thunder,
        no one working could see the rain.

Why aren't the workers memorizing geologic time charts on the job,
        dates of eras and forms of extinction on their fingertips?
Are they bored with the full-length re-runs of their past?
Aren't they happy with a free lifetime supply of dreams?
What ten desert islands have they picked to take with them
        to Megapolis?
I can still hear them saying to each other—
        "It seems I just get out of work and I have to go back."
        or "I look upon it like it's just one big joke."
        or "At least it's not a concentration camp."
Have none of them heard the fog asking to be let in
        to engulf each minion in cool mist?
Does no one remember how they first pronounced
        the Book of Job?
Is no one intoxicated with their philosophy
        of getting high?
Is this death's way of greeting me
        at the beginning of a great career?

## VI

Millions of humans enter factories at dawn.
How many have their arms raised to the sun?
How many want to be late? How many demand to be fired?
Faces leaving as I arrive, faces arriving as I leave—
        It's too easy to say they are zombies.
(Am I not also singing—"I have to go and die some more
        so that my corpse can live"?)

**57**

Even a zombie can think all it makes in its life
        is to some no more than a penny.
Even the daydreams of zombies are full
        of all that cocks and cunts can do.
What does it prove that I can write
        *De mortuis nil nisi bonum*
        on the bags of lids bound for the minsters?

I know I can die without having read any great,
        without having tried sex everyone I found,
        without climbing the highest or sailing the largest alone,
        and without scrawling the great worms of my dreams—
I know life does not care how much we make of it.
Nor does death care, unconcerned with our last words
        or the way we dispose of corpse and grief
        or whether these assumptions are correct
                or whether anyone says—
        "I will worship the spirit of the naked worm
                until death believes in me."
And I know the sun doesn't care if we make our own clothes
        and build our own homes from skins
        of animals we hunt and kill for our food.

When the bombsquad failed to locate the bomb
Someone called up to say would blow up the plant
And the foreman was ordered to order everyone back in,
As the workers returned to drudgery's smithereens
        while kids on summer vacation whizzed by on bicycles
How could I help wishing I'd been the disguised handkerchief
        phoning the bosom to go off?
Ironic, thought I, if this anarchrist explode under me
        as I slaved for the tycoon's cigar!
Suddenly my fingers were once more setting fire
        to miniature models of military reality—
                plastic construction kits of death glued lonely nights

watching horror films on TV—battleships named after states
filled with matchheads and firecrackers
demolished with joy.
Yet what does this prove? Even these inklings can swarm
in the corpse-brains of zombies.


VII


Sometimes I wish there was a log cabin
In the most deafening part of the factory
where I could hermitage
listening to the wind over the chimney,
And every so often as I wrote
peer out through the shade-edge
to see the workers working so hard,
And wonder if they ever figured out
how many lids they touch in a day,
Or if they ever open a can and wonder
if they've already touched it
Or what lips touched what lids
they held in their hands,
Or what they'd think of this poem.
Or if they ever considered the can—
How in 1810 the first can was made,
How the first skilled workers could make
only one by hand an hour,
How today's machines make 1000 a minute,
How America uses 115 million cans each day,
200 billion cans used in the world each year,
Each year enough metal used making cans
to pave a ten-foot-wide highway to the moon!

Soon no one will be left to lift old cans like skulls
to contemplate who quaffed the ravished brides of quietness.

The can-littered streams will remain
        long after America has to be memorized
        by the children of other planets.
Who will remember Continental Can Company
        was the foremost aluminum polluter on earth?
The five billion bacteria in a teaspoon of soil?
The million earthworms per acre?
What bug? What fish? What frog? What snake? What bird?
        What baluchitherium or pteranodon?
                What paleolithic man?
How can I apologize to primeval shorelines cluttered with beercans?
Should I say I needed the money?
Should I say my body is the bible of flies?
Should I say each lid weighs more than an orgasm?
Should I say what if machineroar was rainsong or cricketsong?
Should I say I'm a spy behind enemy lines,
        what top secret will I escape with?
Should I say here's a free pass
        to the antique beercan collector's convention?
Must the beercan on the mountainside
        always be part of the view?


## VIII

Now I understand why one Sunday night
I found myself the only one working in factory,
Given what is not given to every longing for loneliness:
        eight hours of pure underworld,
Eight hours to imagine my life,
Eight hours my machine the only one on
        loud as a bomb continually bursting.
No one knew I imagined myself all ages working there.
No one knew the instant I realized there were 24 presses
        and I was 24 years.

No one asked if I strolled the blackened corridors
         planting a kiss on the jaws of each monster.
No one guessed what the curled emptinesses without ends
            suspended from the ceiling on motionless conveyors
            in both directions to the vanishing point
            might hold for me,
Or the gondolas heaped with punched-out scrap,
Or words Chidiock Tychborn wrote
         the night before the chopping block
         recited by me to the giant metal darkness
         could he ever've imagined?
No one smelled what I smoked in the bathroom stall on my break.
No one saw me write Factories are our churches.
         We worship them more than forests.
         We worship them more than mountains.
         We'd rather drink from the tap than a stream.
         We'd rather open our refrigerator
            than a freshly killed deer.
No one saw me feeling my way back
         through the long dark pillared aisles
            of virgin cans with names we all know.
And when the foreman came by on his yellow scooter
         and from his lips I read LONG NIGHT
What could I do but smile
         for tears to dance round his corpse?

## IX

Am I really from outerspace
Looking through super-x-ray telescope
Observing the life of one earthling
Wondering what it's like being him so much
         my thoughts are the same as his 24 years?
Or is it they captured me when my spaceship landed
            and doped me to forget the planet I'm from
            where I make a million bucks for this poem?

Amazing how they can program robots to imagine!
Making me think I'm alive! Making each memory seem real!
As if I was ever outside the factory even once since I was born!
As if there ever was a first day on the job so eager not to goof up!
Don't they think I can figure it out? Don't they think I know
            science can animate a cadaver? Don't they think I can think
                I've been made to think that I'm human?
Allowing me to flirt with this idea is the key,
        of course, to their control—
                so I can never be sure if they got me.
The sea? The earth? The sky?
They've all been invented for my sake.
There's no History of Life, no Milky Way—
All there is is this factory stretching in every direction forever!
But it's not so bad—at least whatever computer card life
            they give you today really feels like it's happening,
                really feels like the one you've had all along.
And they even let you imagine they've invented some pill
            that'll make you feel while you factory
            that you're foresting or mountaining
            or tasting your first drink from a stream
Or the time and place and life of your choice—
Would you rather be Tyrannosaurus or Teratornis?
Would you rather be Neanderthal or Cro-Magnon?
How about Whitman? You haven't been him for a while.
Or Shakespeare? Remember how much fun it was
            the last time you wrote *Hamlet*?
Aren't you getting tired of discovering the Grand Canyon
            every day for the last two weeks?
Today why not discover fire
            or be Bruckner among the Sequoias?
Today why not yell "I quit!"
            simultaneously in every factory on earth?
Or clap your hands and naked slaves appear
            and dance before your throne!

It's not so bad everyone's aware you're an experiment.
So what if the news runs a continual live broadcast
        of every second of your life?
Be grateful only the most carefully screened geniuses
        are selected to know you,
That everyone you speak to knows their lines in advance,
That even strangers must have degrees in automatonology,
And that right now the scientists are letting you think this.
They laugh. It's part of the hypothesis they're testing:
One of them bends to another and says—"Let's see
        what he says when I turn this knob."

## O HUMAN CANNONBALLS OF EPIPHANY

Can cans ever be canned? Can the can-can ever be canned?
Can cantos of cannonfodder ever be canonized
        or the Canticle of Canticles of Cannabis
        never be cantabiled?
Can canasta in Canada canyons or going to the can
        never be cantata'd
        or can't it be canted
                because of cannibal cancer's uncanny candor
                making even cantaloupes cantankerous?
Hum-drum! Hum-drum! Hum-drum!
I should be paid for discovering America
        is committing suicide with factories!
I should be paid for wondering if I'm only a defect
        in the mass-production of zombies!
I should be paid for pondering if God packages universes
        the way I package lids!
I should be paid for combering if the sea ever gets tired
        of making the same sound!
I should be paid for writing *The Infinite Autobiography*
        *of This Spot Through Eternity!*
I should be paid to stand on this spot
        before America was discovered!

What do I win for singing—"No one can stand where I stand
        because my body is in the way"?
I should be paid to memorize the epic of every split-second!
I should be paid for hearing the chorus of fliptops
        popped all over the globe this instant!
I should be paid for turning fished-out cans upsidedown
        to count how many years falling leaves pour out!
How much do I get for watching the sunrise?
How much do I get for sleeping under the stars?
How much do I get for exploring the undiscovered
        oceans and continents
        and claiming them in Mescaline's name?
How much do these words want to work in my lines?
Is this poem worth more than a skyscraper?
This book worth more moolah than ever made?
I should be paid for listening to music
        better than virtuosos play!
I should be paid to play Kick the Can
        or tie cans to the newlydead's hearse!
I should be paid to fly a kite underground
        careful not to snare it in the roots of trees!
What do I get for sisyphusing my face?
What do I get for glutting my sorrow
        on the wealth of the globèd peonies?
What do I get for knowing the hunting and gathering way of life
        represents 99% man's time on earth?
Or for knowing the slaves who built the pyramids
        carved graffiti praising Pharaoh on the giant blocks
        of stone?
What do I get for knowing a billion dollar bills placed end to end
        would extend four times round the world
        and if you picked them up one per second
        it'd take 134 years?
I should be rich for knowing the answers
        to so many $64,000 Questions!
I should be rich for crying the Tarzan Cry
        that brings the skeletons of extinction to the rescue!

Before, I said—"There will always be room in my brain
          for the universe!"
Before, I said—"My soul will never be bludgeoned
          by the need to make money!"
Before, I said—"I will never cringe under the crack
          of the slavedriver's whip!"
Now my job is to murder the oceans!
Now my job is to poison the air!
Now my job is to chop down every tree!
I make food full of poison and say—"This is what you must buy!"
I'm in charge of torturing heretics
          and anyone who disagrees with the king!
I spend eight hours a day crucifying saviors!
I spend eight hours a day executing Lorcas!
I make slag heaps out of human souls!
I'm the first to go in the gas chamber after it's all over.
The corpses are piled on top of each other,
          the strongest on top, the weakest on bottom,
          all naked, many still twitching, still bleeding
                    from noses and mouths,
          vomit, shit and piss befouling the agonied postures.
My job is to pull the gold teeth
          and shovel the bodies into the ovens.
Thanks to my work, Wolf Grizzly Eagle Whale
          and other deities in the pantheon of pantheism
                    are no longer a threat to organized religion.
My job is to drop the Atomic Bomb on Hiroshima.
Twenty years later, asked would I do it again
          I say—"Yes."

O pay me for receiving the prophecies
          of the maggots of other worlds!
Pay me for the planets where before I was born
          I sang lullabies from my mother's vagina!

**65**

Let me be paid for bringing into Poetry
        penises and vaginas that will give us the visions
            we have wanted them to all along!
Let me be paid for rolling up my shirtsleeves and worshipping
        the ejaculations of joy!
O I should be paid to give blowjobs to boys,
        one hundred a day for the rest of my life!
And girls should be tickled pink for me to lick their cunts
        till flying saucers come with frankincense and myrrh!
Eureka! I will make my fortune from plagiarizing death!
I will take the words from its mouth and it will not care!
I should be paid to say everyone's job is enlightenment!
I should be paid to run naked through the sprinkler
        the hottest day of summer!
I should be paid to lie in a canoe
        and drift over the lake all day!
What does it profit me to discover the pyramid
        of cans in the supermarket?
I demand to know how much sphincter gets
        staring brown daggers at its reflection!
How many smackers the tuckered-out eardrums?
How many frogskins the herculean heart
        and hardworking gonads?
Where are my royalties for discovering the telephone?
        And didn't I invent applause?
How many yachts and racehorses is that worth?
How many mansions? How many limousines
        for going over the Niagara of Last Words on a tightrope?
O pay me for saying if 75 feet represents the age of the earth
        each step I take equals 100 million years!
O pay me for saying I could live the rest of my life
        on the money it costs to make one 500-pound bomb!
O pay me for saying every five days one million more humans
        on planet!
O pay me for discovering the origin of writing
        was to keep track of wealth and slaves!

O pay me for saying children who worked 12 hours a day
            were so tired they fell asleep with food in their mouths!
O pay me for showing adults in factories
            as tragic as child labor!
O pay me eight hours a day to do nothing
            but make bombscare phonecalls!
O pay me to say a poem is the best way
            to blow up a factory!
How many mediums of exchange do I get
            for getting higher than ever?
The cry of the eagle gives me a million!
The taste of wild berries gives me a million!
The smell of black locusts gives me a million!
The feeling swimming naked gives me a million!
I'm rich with all the visions opening cocoons afford!
A billionaire of reincarnations that can never be bankrupt!
O pay me to dress up as Santa
            and go down the Auschwitz chimneys!
O pay me for using so many exclamation points!
            Each worth more than a skyscraper!
O pay me for crushing a can in each fist!
Workaday! Workaday! Workaday!
Pilfer your livelong life away!
How can I think of quittin when dis is moh fuhn
            dhan goin down da Big Muddy on a raf wif a runaway?


I guess I should tell you I'm really a zillionaire
            doing slave work just to see what it's like—
Or wait a minute, is it that I took some drug
            that makes me think I'm a zillionaire who took some drug
            to forget he's a zillionaire to see what doing slave
                work is like?


O pay me for knowing they let me say this.
For picturing how the control panel in robotfactory headquarters
            reacts,

How it flashes and the dials jump when I say
            the scientists are pleased with their creation.
One of them reads from the tickertape each word as I write it.
"Hey, listen to this," he smirks—
"I should be paid to say death restores us to soil
            no matter how unenlightened we are:
All melt in the mouth of the earth:
Each one is scrumptious to the critters
            to whom corpses taste good:
Each corpse a gift to the ground
            for roots to open into everything beyond them,
Opening slowly as the Colorado unwrapped the Grand Canyon
            till once more you're dreaming of gifts beneath the tree:
So don't bother complimenting death.
            Flattery will get you nowhere."
The scientists can't keep from clapping.
One of them bends to another and whispers—
            "Remember when he raved about the laureate of blowjobs?"
"No, but is it true he said he got lost
            counting all the boyhoods he had?"


                              X


O thinking so much makes me weary.
Maybe I should pretend the masters
Nodding their heads in the invisible auditorium
            in which continual dialogues are held
            on the progress of my computerized soul
                  are only a dream.
Maybe if I just stop thinking and look at the machines—
            the way the lids pour out like suicide battalions,
            the way I pretend to check for defects every so often,
            the way I shove enough in the bag like this,
            the way I stand the filled bag on end like this,
            the way I fold over the top and tape it like this,
            the way the rows of 'em rise on the skid like this—

MMMMMM, that's better, now I'm myself again—
All I have to do is stand here
        and package factories as they come from the press—
Factories that make cans.
Factories that make the machines that make cans.
Factories that make the machines that make the machines
        that make cans.
Factories that make factories.
Factories that make factories that make factories
        that make everything that goes into cans.
Factories that make canopeners.
Factories that make electric canopeners.
Factories that make candy and canoes.
Factories that make candles and candelabras
        and incandescent lightbulbs.
Factories that make cuckoo-clock canaries.
Industries of canned laughter, canned applause,
        canned music.
Telephone factories, television factories,
        radio, stereo, tape recorder factories,
        refrigerator, stove and toilet factories.
Telescope factories, microscope factories,
        film, camera, movie screen factories,
        jukebox, roulette wheel and slot machine factories.
Industries of nuts! Industries of bolts!
Industries of bulldozers, roadgraders, steamshovels,
        cement mixers, steamrollers, jackhammers,
        pile drivers and wrecking cranes!
Every building and street in every dot on the map
        and all the highways between them
        constructed from products of multitudinous factories!
Factories of cars and toy cars,
        trucks and toy trucks, trains and toy trains,
        planes and toy planes, ships and toy ships,
        spaceships and toy spaceships!
Factories of money and factories of play money!

**69**

Factories of all that money can buy!
Mass production of pricetags!
Assembly lines of cash registers!
Application and paycheck form factories!
Lunchbucket and thermosbottle factories!
Earplug and timeclock and alarmclock factories!
           and self-winding watches given factoryhands at retirement
           made in what factories!
Factories of lady's ware, men's ware, children's ware, baby's ware,
           silverware, copperware, tinware, glassware,
           stoneware, woodenware, earthenware, plasticware,
           furniture, souvenirs, knickknacks, novelties,
           gizmos, geegaws, glockenspiels and greeting cards!
Ambulances, police cars, and buses from factories!
Fire engines, fire escapes, and matches from factories!
Sirens, foghorns, steamwhistles, rockguitars, grandpianos,
           every instrument in the orchestra including the baton
           and the concert hall all hatched from myriad factories!
O every record I love I know where you come from!
O cookiecutters! birdhouses! buddhastatues and plastic vomit!
     I know where you come from!
           O awls, axes, adzes, augers,
           barrels, bearings, bellows, brads,
           crowbars, corkscrews, crucibles, calipers,
           dumbbells, dollies, dibbles, drills,
           exhausts, excelsior, forceps, faucets,
           gauges, gouges, gaskets, goggles,
           hammers, hammocks, hangers, hoists,
           irons, icepicks, jewels, jacks,
           keels, kilns, levels, ladles, lathes,
           mops, muzzles, mattresses, microphones,
           nails, neon, napalm, ouija boards,
           pistons, pitchforks, pliers, puncheons,
           quivers, quoits, ratchets, rounces,
           radar, roachclips, scales, scalpels,
           snorkels, stencils, shovels, shoetrees,

squeegees, tweezers, trophies, trocars,
tampons, trampolines, uniforms, umbrellas,
vises, valves, wormgears, wrenches,
wigs, wire, yardsticks, zippers—
I know where you come from!
And I know where the machines that make you come from!
And all the letters for alphabet soup!
Breweries, canneries, tanneries, creameries,
(Name me something not come from Factory)
Brassworks, gasworks, refineries, binderies,
Plants that make barberpoles, barberchairs,
dentistchairs, electric chairs,
electric knives, electric fans,
electric shavers, electric blenders,
electric blankets, electric fireplaces,
electric toothbrushes, electric eyes!
*Everything in the Sears Roebuck Catalogue*
*is not from the legendary herds of buffalo!*
Typewriter sweatshops! Motorcycle sweatshops!
Revolving door sweatshops! Intercom sweatshops!
Mass production of straitjackets!
Mass production of bombs!
Vast spectrum of death machines of land, sea and sky!
More bullets than people who ever lived!
More bayonets than books ever written!
Better machines for killing invented so fast
they're obsolete before used!
So much an hour mass production of crosses and flags!
Purple-heart gristmills! Basket-case gristmills!
Industries of homicidal deceit:
glamorizing cigarets no different than Nazis
telling Jews gas chambers are shower rooms!
Millions of new cradles and coffins each year!
Corpses rolling down the conveyor belt of the funeral factory!
Slaughterhouse factories and all the tools of the slaughterhouse:
cleavers, bludgeons, meat-hooks, sticklers!

Fish, mammal, bird factories! Fruit, vegetable, grain factories!
        Every bite processed in factories!
Strip me naked, abandon me in deepest woods in Canada—
        my body still from Factory!
My flesh flesh of what factories raised from birth
        and murdered for my mouth!
Supermarket Factories! University Factories!
Hospital Factories! Prison Factories!
        Death Factories!
Stop! Don't you think I get the point?
All the floors of the department store
        and the elevator girl telling me
                the goods on each as the doors open?
Is it necessary to list
        every machine necessary to extract raw materials
        and every machine necessary to transport them
        and every machine necessary to transform them
                into iron, steel, aluminum,
        and everything made from iron, steel, aluminum,
        and every machine necessary to make it?
What do I get for unveiling the machinery that makes
        footballs, baseballs, basketballs, tennisballs,
        bowlingballs, billiardballs, pingpongballs, snowmobiles,
        boxinggloves, golfclubs, sailboats, surfboards,
        scubagear, bathtubs, and easychairs?
Must we see the slaves behind every device of recreation and leisure?
Must we see the slaves behind every laborsaving device?
(Do you think it's trite to call them slaves?
Are you only a company man for Literature
        slaving on the disassembly line of criticism?
Are you only a cog in the Poetry Factory?
How many poems by Zinjanthropus
        appear in your Immortal Anthology?)
Wheelbarrow factories! Kitchen sink capitalisms!
Staplegun generalissimos! Toothpick presidents!

Paperclip czars! Linoleum pharaohs!
Punchpress emperors! Pushbutton potentates!
Monopoly millionaires! Deodorant billionaires!
Electricity trillionaires! Computer quadrillionaires!
Quintillionaires of wood! Sextillionaires of rock!
Septillionaires of plastic! Octillionaires of oil!
Nonillionaires of flesh! Decillionaires of Oblivion!
      The exact number of pennies ever made!
      The exact number of papercups ever made!
      The exact number of number two pencils ever made!
More rope! More tape! More pipe! More fence!
More wallets! More purses! More needles! More thread!
More envelopes! More stamps! More brushes! More paint!
More boxes! More bottles! More screws! More screwdrivers!
More washingmachines! More airconditioners! More vacuum cleaners!
      More flashlight batteries!
Dynamos stretching to the horizon and still not enough!
More generators! More blastfurnaces! More concrete! More antennae!
Capitalisms of thumbtacks and thumbscrews!
Stockholders in tongue-depressors and rectal thermometers!
Manufacturers of lawnmowers, snowblowers, toenail clippers
      and machetes!
World's largest producers of arrows, slingshots, fishhooks,
      riflesights, decoys, traps, and raccoon death-cry calls!
Peddlers of pills and more pills and pill containers
      and prescription forms!
Industries for the Blind! Industries for the Retarded!
Where artificial flavor and color are made!
Where artificial flowers and grass are made!
Where artificial eyes and arms and legs are made!
      and wherever they make boobytraps!
      and wherever they make tiddlywinks!
      and wherever they make doors and doorknobs
         and doorbells and hinges and locks and keys!
Corporations of bulletproof vests and silencers!

Corporations of blowtorches, rivetguns and girders!
(And where do dildoes and bathyspheres fit in?)
Every breath more parkingmeters and bankvaults
            and armored trucks and turnstiles
            and wedding rings and vagina dolls
            and rubbers and rubberbands
            and rubber rafts and lifepreservers
            and thingamabobs and thingamadoodles
            and gargle and garbage trucks
                and garbage cans
                and sprinkling cans
                and aerosol cans
                and "Eat" signs
                and "Stop" signs
                and "No Trespassing" signs
            and switchboards and turbines
            and conveyor belts of conveyor belts!
And the world's largest producers of machineguns and chainsaws!
And 20,000 a day extermination factory of Auschwitz!
And one billion gallons of gasoline burned in California each month!
And 38 cigarets inhaled every day in New York City
            just by breathing the air!
And even you, backpacks, compasses, and maps of the wild?
            must you be from factories?
*Et tu* mountain climbing gear?
And even icecream and kaleidoscopes
            and bubblewands and balloons
                and swingsets and teetertotters
                and yoyos and marbles
                and frisbees and skateboards
                and pinwheels and merrygorounds
                and beanies with propellers
                and the hall of mirrors?
Must we see the slaves behind every toy of our childhood?
Must we see the gypped lives behind the pantheon of laughs?

O souls flophoused by factories!
O geniuses imbeciled by factories!
O enlightenment shoplifted by factories!
Copying machine factories! Calculating machine factories!
Vending machine factories! Change machine factories!
Humans spending their lives making lipstick or eyeshadow!
Humans spending their lives making crystal balls or fortune cookies!
Humans spending their lives making calendars or blindman canes!
Working your way up to foreman in the insecticide factory!
Working your way up to employment manager in the squirtgun factory!
Working your way up to the top in the pay toilet factory!
 40 years making piggybanks!
 480 months making burglar alarms or handcuffs!
 2000 weeks making wind chimes, wind machines
  or wind-up toys!
 10,400 days of your life
  making stopwatches or metronomes!
 83,200 hours of your life
  making miniature replicas of Rodin's Thinker!
 4,992,000 minutes of your life
  gluing the hemispheres of globes together!
 299,952,000 seconds of your life
  cranking out the links of chains!

XI

What have I forgotten?
How many more should I name?
Is there no end to this list?
Factories that make newspapers every day
 and all the job openings in the want ads?
Factories that make yellow pages and all the factories
 in the yellow pages of every city on earth?
More factories than words in this poem!
More than all the odes in praise of marijuana or blowjobs
 ever written!

More than all the miles I'll ever backpack or canoe
            pristine primordial lake-forest-peak wilderness!
Even if I toured every factory there is
            and each tour lasted only a minute,
            it would take centuries!
No second of my life in which slaves are not slaving!

Don't tell me it's trite to say they are slaves!
Don't tell me it's banal to say every second counts!
Don't tell me I use too many exclamation points!
(Can there ever be too many exclamation points!)
Don't tell me it's boring to see all the ways
            humans make human sacrifice of their lives!
Don't tell me how leaves are factories!
            or of the factories of my bones and balls!
I have milked by hand! I know the milking machine joke!
I know I smell with an olfactory system!
I know mitochondria are the power houses of cells!
I don't need to be reminded honey is the busywork of bees!
I don't need to be told the Sun is the Factory of Light!

Death from the cornucopia of Factories!
Death from the stupor, stupor, stupor of the daily grind!
Massacre of land, sea and sky by stupendous machines!
Mutilation of souls beyond recognition!
Factories that have actually made enough bombs
            to blow up the Earth any second!
Factories of the death-cry of America and Mankind
            and every Livingkind on my planet!
Factories whose noise numbs the ear to Poetry!
Factories whose God is not Love unless Love is Money!
Factories that make millions of books that say—
            "Without factories we couldn't live.
Behind everything we need to survive is a machine.
Without factories you wouldn't be reading these words."

I draw lines from all the things I own
          to the factories that made them
          and from each factory to the homes of its slaves.
How long will it take me to work my whole life
          on each of the jobs in every factory on earth?
Ah, epics could be written in each of them.
How would this all be different
          if I'd worked where they make
               kites or fireworks,
               teaballs or plumbbobs,
               mannikins or sledgehammers,
               tuning forks or cattleprods,
               flamethrowers or shoppingcarts,
               wheelchairs or hearingaids,
               paper or fountain pens,
               pacifiers or puppets,
               or poured sand into hourglasses
               passing by on conveyor belt?

Maybe I won't be able to write unless I work in a factory!
Even if I get rich I'll have to buy a machine
          for the turret of my castle
               so I can go there and scribble
               to its ravenous roar:
Except to make money,
We are no longer responsible for our survival.
We don't have to hunt or kill our own food.
We don't have to build our own houses or tools,
          know how to make fire without matches,
               make our own clothes or canoes,
               be our own heroes, doctors, priests,
          and teach our children how to smell the weather.
Once there were no cities or farms.
Once there were no factories or slaves.
Once everything ever made in factories did not exist.

Is there no way to cut the umbilicus to factories?
No way to be born into a world not made in factories?
No way to unpledge this hopeless allegiance
        to suicide by factories?
Not one stream left where the water flows free
        of human junk from source to mouth?
No breath left to breathe anywhere
        untainted by exhaust pipes and smokestacks?
Is it too late to ask—"What good is it if we're immortal
        when we're bored with eternity even before we die?"
Is it time to begin to dream of the sphere in space
        where America exists before it was discovered?
What was I born for? What was I born for?
        Is this a Factory I see before me?


                        XII


Perhaps you've already stopped reading this poem,
Perhaps you want to get paid for reading this far.
Don't think I haven't caught you turning the pages
        to see how much longer it is to the end.
Don't think I haven't caught you
        looking at the clock.
How long does it take to write *I am growing old?*
What right do 24 years have to speak of age?

This poem does not want to die,
        but it is very tired now.
It has so many little children in it
        that want to go home,
That want to be told a story
        they can fall asleep halfway through—

Once, that day before the night I worked alone,
        past "No Trespassing" signs and barbed wire,
Smoking the last words of centuries
        amid birch, oak, shagbark and grosbeak song,

Exhaling into faces of trilliums and mosquitos,
          wanting everything to be high,
In a small clearing I did what I always wanted to do—
          stripped naked and shat—
My head and arms rising to the sun
          so that when they could reach no further
I felt what my body would never be again touch me for the last time,
          smelling in the 93 million mile rays my remains,
               my source,
And savoring the mystic perfume in that stench
(Perfume that can be called nothing but mystic)
And grabbing myself as if my hand were God
I pulled my life from my testicles up and out
          the shaft of my blazing erection—
               splendid arcs of semen
               glittering through the air—
Saying to my turds—"Be my past, be my boyish boyhoods
          small shap't and firmly carv'd, finely laid and sleek,"
And to my semen—"Be my future, my future opening mouth
          between legs spread with naked joy
          in the wavering leaf-shade
          where Indian Pipes and Moccasin Flowers
          are still fringed with dew."
An hour later Factory surrounded me.
A week later pilgrimage found no trace of my conversion.

## XIII

What more can I say?
The day came as I knew it would,
The day that waited for me all along
          just as much as the machines waited,
Just as much as the day I was conceived
And all the days before I had to become a slave,
          before I was taught to spell money,
Before I understood my corpse

**79**

and everything beyond the disappearance of my corpse
     waits for me,
And just as much as the end of this poem
Waited for me before the beginning of time
    and for whoever reads it
       after the extinction of clocks,
The day I would quit waited for me,
Waited for me to apply and be hired,
For the routines of slavery to be learned
    and the slow countdown of days
       to be endured,
For me, it waited, patiently, that day,
Waited for me to pick up my paycheck so many times,
To stare at the clock as I worked dreaming of quitting
    so many times,
To think of all the things as a man I did not want to be,
And for freedom to long for me patient as worms
    all the days before they are human again,
While the odyssey of eternity on this one spot in the universe
    contemplated itself—
While the infinite epic of each second in infinity
    touched me—
From the birth of the sun,
From the birth of the earth,
From the birth of all life
    to the earliest men,
From the discovery of fire,
From the invention of tools,
From when each word was once a poem
    and what it was like to live at that time
       when all men hunted and killed their own food
       and carved the mammoth from the mammoth's tusk,
From the invention of farming and herding 10,000 years ago,
From the invention of writing 5000 years ago
    and printing 500 years ago,
From the first cities, from the first factories,

From the first swirl of the whirlpool
        whose vortex we spin in so fast
            no one knows anymore what will happen,
From having to stop writing these words every ten seconds
        to tube or bag the lids of cans
And how this incantation rose and still rises
        and will never stop rising
            from the catacombs of incomprehensible zombies!
And so, as I knew it would, the day came
When waiting in line to punch out it was for the last time,
When for the last time I would see the slaves
        race past me trying to be first
            from carlot to freeway to bar
        to drink till they dreamed they were free,
When for the last time I would follow the way home
        past all the factories that lay between
            giant in the aura of their power at midnight
        through the empty streets in the rain.

How could I have known months after I quit
        as I lay waiting for sleep
            my ears would still echo that roar,
        the din of presses and minsters?
How could I have known I'd bolt from bed at all hours
        gasping—"I'm late!"
            only to realize I quit long ago
        the din of presses and minsters?
How could I have known years later driving past Factory
        the most seductive night of summer,
            seeing all the lights on, the smokestacks billowing,
        I would say—"Just think, people are working right now"
            and let the best grass I ever smoked
        remember me there
            in the din of presses and minsters?

*How can you kill yourself if you're already dead?*

*How can you kill yourself with something made in a factory?*
*How can you kill yourself before embracing the invisible tree*
        *above every stump?*
*How can you kill yourself before the arena*
        *packed with your future lives*
        *cheers you on?*
Before, I said—"If you've already stopped reading this
        you'll never know how it ends!"
Before, I said—"As long as there are slaves
        this poem will never end!
        As long as there are factories
        my metamorphosed remains
        will continue to ponder
        the wasted lives!"
Before, I said—"Poets should be paid to skydive naked
        to all the doors where slaves go in,
            proclaiming from the robes of their chutes
        how the corpse waits in the man
        the man waits in the boy
        the boy waits in the child
        the child waits in the baby
            waiting all the orgasms of ancestors
            to be fucked into being
        patient as maggots are patient
        all the days they must wait
            before they become human again,
        before they elegize again the wasted lives,
        before they can proclaim once more
            the immortality of death!"

What am I waiting for? I am free to go.
The next shift has begun. Why am I standing here
        watching them work?
There's nothing I can say they will hear.
There's nothing more to be seen.
I have shown the gouged-out souls.

I have shown the castrated souls.
I have shown the souls torn limb from limb.
I have shown the disemboweled souls.
Now you know the difference between hunting for money
          and hunting the woolly rhinoceros.
I have performed the adagio of the opening cocoon.
Because of me Poetry knows my childhood
          stacked coins into dank castles of smell.
Because of me Poetry knows it took 500 million man-hours
          to build the highest building in the world.
Because of me from now on every factory-made object
          unceasingly mantras—"I was made by a slave!"
I have not made my fortune in gravedigging machines
          or garbage disposals.
I'm no plutonium tycoon or entrepreneur of nerve gas.
I'll never spend my life creating ways to make poison taste better
          and sell more.
From mountaintops I have gazed
          more than the money of all time.
From the start the rainbow has arched to my palate
          the promise of these words.
I have inherited the earth.
I have inherited the sky.
I have tinkered this handmade craftsmanship
          in my own little shop.
The Epic of Zombies has come from my hand.
The Spectacle of Millions Slowly Tortured to Death Their Whole Lives
          has come from my hand.
There aren't enough libraries for the screams.
There aren't enough banks for the tears.
Can't you smell the putrescent lives?
The wasted lives, can't you smell them?
I've escaped unburied from the untold miles of genocide tickertape
          gibbered from the monoliths of greed.
I've escaped from the slaughterhouse of souls.

I've closed my eyes by the machines
        and imagined I stood in the thunder and spray
        of the unknown falls
Crying—"Every city that exists will disappear!
        Every nation that exists will disappear!"
Don't ask me how. Don't ask me why.
All I know is numberless planets
        have realized Utopia.
All I know is there will be no ghost dance
        for the nuclear bomb.
All I know is no one will timemachine to our time
        to work in a tollway tollbooth
            giving correct change their whole life
        to car after car.

O millions of sanddollars be left by the tide!
O children radiant with soot emerge from the mines at last!
O inside the pyramid stand on the spot where you look up
        and see through to the stars!
Freedom! Liberty! Deliverance!
(Am I the primitive man who invented those words?)
I proclaim the resurrection of everyone who is dead
        that is still alive!
No one will have giant keys in their backs any longer!
No one will cut themselves and find clockwork inside any longer!
From now on no one will die discovering they had not lived!
        No more strangleholds! No more strangleholds!
Ungag our souls!! Unstrangle our souls!! Unsmother our souls!!
        I PROCLAIM THE EXTINCTION OF FACTORIES!!!
Already they are gone. Not a trace remains.
        I can hardly believe I am so powerful.
There are no more slaves! No one knows anymore what money is!
The utmost passion of eternity feels itself in every human being!
        Everything ever made in factories has disappeared.
Once more a squirrel can travel from the Atlantic to the Mississippi
        from tree to tree without touching the ground.

Once more the buffalo and passenger pigeon.
Once more wilderness earth that is heaven.
Once more wilderness men that are gods.
I gaze down on the untouched continent.
How many centuries have fallen away?
            Is this America?
                    What should I call it?
Am I the first man
            to set foot
                    on this land?


Here is the door.
I'll open it now.
All I have to do
            is open it
            and leave.
For all I know
            the city will no longer be there
            and I'll walk into the absolute forest—
Machines are not trees, machines are not clouds,
Lids advancing forever are neither streams nor lapping shores,
Clocks are not moons, moons are not coins,
Coins are not the view from the mountaintop,
            jobs are not sunrise,
            work is not dawn:
The Miracle of Factory passes from my life!
"Working at Continental Can Co." R!I!P!


Like a kite played higher and higher
Pulls more gently as it gets smaller and smaller
            until it's hardly there, only a dot,
                    and tugs like the memory
            of some unrequited caress,
So the years have come between me and that time,
            those factorydays of my past,
                    those futile days of my life,

But not until all factories are turned into playgrounds in moonlight,
Not until all applicants for factories must memorize this poem
       to be hired,
Not until I'm hired to dress like a grasshopper and fiddle
      "O the world owes me a livin' "
         to the nation of ants
Will I let go of the string.

And when the time comes to let go
Let the last thing I remember be
      the night when the power failed,
When the monsters that even now
      are preaching the same circular words
        that will outlive us all failed,
When everything stopped and went dark,
How in the sudden vast silence of factory
      I heard my own voice for the first time,
And crouching at the feet of the machines
In that dark broken only by exit lights
      how I closed my eyes
Wondering if when I opened them
      I would be 15,000 years ago
Beginning in the flickering of my torch
      to paint the antler'd dancer
         on the vault of my cave.

# FIRST
# DRINK
# FROM A
# STREAM

# The Puberty of Smell

If the second before pulling the trigger you remember me,
      remember me smelling lilacs,
How every time smelling lilacs I remember
The time my mescalined olfactory system
         caught on the early morning breeze
         the full-blossomed and blossoming lilacs
            at Big Smoky Falls,
How my nose approached like a boy
         discovering his cock feels so good
         he can't help crying out,
How circling the tree at nose level
         caressing with my nose
         those purple clouds of fragrance
I experienced where I smell inside my skull
         above my mouth and under my eyes
            in the very center
         my nose's first orgasm,
Not caring if anyone saw my abandon—
Though no one was there, no one but birds
         and songs the sun rises in them
            and the falls and the song of the falls
         and the song of mosquitos
            I gave my blood to with joy—
And even if I didn't think then
         of the scent between pubescent legs,
Or remember my boyhood cock no longer exists
         to caress breasts of early morning dreams,
I saw them opening,
         all opening and opening themselves
And glowing in the sun's first rays,
         lifting themselves to the sun
         in the just-felt breeze

As if they'd waited,
As if everything in the Universe had waited
Till I came, till I could smell them opening,
        my nose caressed by those blossoms, those lilacs,
        those clusters of fragrance and the living color
            called purple,
As I opened and closed my eyes with my breathing,
Every so often remembering where I was,
Remembering I had a face and that face had a nose—
        for didn't it seem to me then
        all I was was that smell?


Jim—
Even if you've already killed yourself,
When the time comes you have my name and I have yours,
        write this for me,
Or when next you're about to pull the trigger,
Remember in that second before you discover
        if you can hear the shot
That for a few grains of the hourglass
        this was me—
That I too had no choice,
        drawn by the smell irresistible,
My nose approaching like the lover
        who believes no one on earth can love
            more passionately—
Remember me then smelling so hard
As if I were the first to aroma
        this peculiar translation of corpses,
As if I were the first to make love to lilacs,
As if I were entering strange houses of early morning
        drawn toward sleeping boys to hold lilac sprigs
        to nostrils of their dreams,
As if I'd discovered the answer
        to all the questions the Universe inside my skull
        could ask.

And so, in the second before you blow out your brain,
        when you look into the gun and feel
           where the hole in your head will be,
Remember you were immortal before you were born,
        that even before this poem
           your suicide must be fragrant as lilacs,
And always remember in that morning the color of lilacs,
How I smelled them till I could smell them no more,
        withdrawing, fulfilled and wondering
If you went to those lilacs at Big Smoky Falls
        you'd be surprised they had no smell
        because I must've inhaled it all,
Wondering if I'd smelled those purple clouds so well
        if you inhaled from my nose
        you could smell them now.

# Refugee

Remember, poets, when you wage a poem against war,
        you need paper,
Trees must be cut by slaves, trucked by slaves,
        pulped and sold by slaves
        for the green paper that enslaves us all,
And under your pen the paper struggles to escape,
        not wanting to be cut down again.
It knows it can't help break the silence
        with whatever you force it to confess.
And don't forget the war poets wage against each other,
At readings how many hope their poems will defeat
        the poems of the others?
And published in magazines, each poem a medal, a promotion,
        a notch on the barrel.
The waking student, who cares more for who turns to him in bed
        than anything, glances at your works,
        sure he can remember the name,
        the passwords,
This one means this, that that....

Soon the young will have to memorize the names and dates
        of this war.
After the murder of one hundred million in less than
        one hundred years
What do we desire? Peace?
There are so many wars, I think each of them
        is a word in the dictionary.
There are so many wars, I think each of them
        is a human being.
On tombstones I read the dates of the wars.
I want to get so far away
        war can cease to exist
        as long as I live.

I want to hide somewhere in the mountains for fifty years,
       and then, but for one day only,
       come back and find everything
Changed, for better or worse,
       but knowing I will never return again.

## Grace

When you no longer thank God for flesh set before you,
When not even silence preludes the toil of jaws,
Or when eating alone you turn on the radio
  because the noise your face makes
  makes you uncomfortable,
You could be graced with a vision that comes
  like the visions that come to those who've chosen
  to eat only their hunger.
And if then you say we should kill what we eat,
  kill what we eat so we know who to thank
  hearing cries butchered animals make,
So we can point out on our own bodies
  where this meat comes from,
I'd say: It's not enough to become the one
  who hammers cow brains or stickles upsidedown pigs,
Not enough to eat from china designed with pictures
  of slaughterhouse,
Not even enough to know why Chippewa cut open just-killed doe
  to partake the fresh excrement,
Or how Sioux boys kissed the first fish
  throwing him back to tell the rest it was alright
  because they asked to be forgiven,
Or that "We can't live without killing"
  can't be said too many times,
Or that to count out loud the number of lambs
  gone to the supermarket during the last war
  would take longer than we have to live,
Or that garbage from all the suppers of one day in America
  would stem the hungers that have cried for so long
  they've lost their voice.
None of this is enough. A God has said
  we must kill with our mouth,

Our eyes must be that close to what makes us survive,
    what keeps our lips worthy of the long kisses
    in which the tongue passes along the edges of a girl's teeth.

## The Dark Inside a Life

To learn how to die cut down a tree,
Watch how so many years fall.
You don't need to have planted it for it to be your life.

You know countless trees have grown
        and will grow where this tree falls.
Everyone alive now will be underground
        and will have gone from roots, branches and leaves
        to roots, branches and leaves many times.
You've seen how the seed of a tree
        can rise from the pit of a stump.
Wherever your feet touch earth
        you know you are touching
        where something has died or been born.

Count the rings and stand on the stump and stretch your arms
        to the sky.
Think only because it was cut down could you do this.
*You are standing where no one has stood*
        *but the dark inside a life*
        *that many years.*

# View from Imp Lake Lookout

Before taking Mescaline at Imp Lake
I drove up the dirt road to the lookout the map told me was there
To find only the platform where it stood remained,
And standing where the tower once stood,
        looking up being my view,
It seemed the lifetime of the tower and the tower's view
        and all the feet that ever climbed the winding stairs to the top
        imagined me then:
The ranger deciding here was the spot for the tower,
The tower in the architect's brain, the factory fashioning its parts,
The shipment of parts, the making of the forest road
        and the Tower signpost and parkinglot
        and path from parkinglot to the tower's base,
And the tower's construction, the unfolding blueprint,
        trees falling, girders rising, putting in the steps,
        securing the viewing platform, the foreman's final OK,
        machinery and workers driving away, the money it cost
        changing hands, the silence returning once more,
And all the feet that climbed the lifespan of the tower—
        how many years how many footsteps echoing upward
        toward the vista expanding in every direction
        each footstep up the number of steps upward
        50, 100, 150, 200 feet high,
Dawn, noon, dusk, night, spring, summer, fall, winter,
        the continual autobiography of the sky—
Babies carried up in their mothers' arms,
Children who can climb only one step at a time,
Girls two steps at a time racing friends to the top
        nonstop giggling out-of-breath,
Boys on top holding the gobbing contest or the pissing contest
        or balancing on guard rails on a dare,
Fathers yelling at kids to be careful,

Those afraid to go all the way up,
Those too old reading "Climb at your own risk"
        who climb up anyway,
Those gone to the top for blowjob in moonlight,
        or fucking in sunrise,
Those curious what makes pretending to throw each other off
        so much fun,
Epileptics, amputees, morons, deformed persons, those who are blind,
        and fetuses umbilicusing the view from their mothers' eyes,
Those blindfolded by friends, not told where they're going,
        led to the top and the blindfold unpinned,
And those who looked from the top but never really saw the view,
All walks of life walking upward, all different outlooks looking out,
All the occupations in the yellow pages rising above the trees
        and the dream of the job that's living on a tower
        and looking for fires rising with them,
And those lamenting the extinction of crow's-nests, lighthouses
        and lookout towers,
And the one wondering if someday the tower will stand
        surrounded by rushhour megapolis
        (quaint reminder of Upper Michigan wilds
        extant in the shadow of highrise apartments),
And the one wondering how long to stay on top
        because friends are restless and want to move on,
And the one who believes himself unworthy to go up
        till all the woods seen from the view have walked through him,
And don't forget the one who goes up to see what the forest
        that'll take Mescaline in him looks like to a hovering bird,
And don't forget Mescaline climbing the tower
        in the shape of a human being,
And don't forget Mescaline climbing steps of epiphany
        in the human brain,
And connoisseurs of wilderness towers
        who pilgrimage from towertop to towertop,
Those who like being noisy on top,
Those to whom even a whisper is sacrilege,

And all who returned again and again,
Who climbed these winding stairs each year of their life,
Who became friends with the view
        and gloried in the possibilities of Tower—
Sunrise on top, Sunset on top,
        star study, cloud study, bird study on top,
Thanksgiving on top, kite flying on top,
        milkweedpods, waterballoons, soapbubbles on top,
        snowmen on top, trampoline on top, tai chi or yoga
        or Auschwitz photos on top, flute or harp
        or helicoptered piano on top, photography on top,
        topography on top, Mescaline on top,
        soliloquy on top, suicide on top,
        jacking off on top in berserk thunderstorm,
Shouting your name loud as you can from cupped hands
        and cupping your ears for an echo,
Learning the view by heart,
Dancing the view turning in circles fast as you can,
Scribbling "inexhaustible view" in your notebook
        or "the vista that invites the eye into its distance"
        or "the panorama expanding before me further than I can see,"
Dropping a boulder from on top close as possible
        to your friend's head as he lies on the ground watching it fall
        to savor the shock of his body hitting the ground if he jumped,
Smearing the steps with honey and dressing in clothes made of bacon
        crouched on top for the dream-bear,
Or wearing costumes of other times and lands as you climb,
        or smoking a joint each step of the way,
Or digging secret passageway from the tower's base to your basement,
Or performing the ceremony of climbing in fog
        when from the base the top of the tower is lost
        and when from the top not even the tops of trees can be seen,
And all those wilderness tourists who considered the tower their throne,
        anyone else there a trespasser on their solitude kingdom,
And how many times hoping to find no one there,
        on reaching the last breathless step
        someone's already conducting the view from the podium,

And finally, the poet who imagined me writing this poem,
        who looked down where I stand now looking up . . .
And so, looking up at the towerless sky,
        I wondered,
Is this all that's left of the view?

(If there is an audience and I'm reading this
        it should be from a tower.
In a room if this poem succeeds,
        walls become lakes, chairs become trees,
        200 feet of tower rise me above them,
        ceiling becomes sky and I'm alone once more
And each of you is alone on some wilderness dream-risen tower.)

But the map still shows the tower is there
And I keep seeing the others who will drive up the dirt road
Only to look up from the base the tower was secured to and rested on
Wishing for the view the top commanded
        to command them
From days no one was there and the view could enjoy being alone,
Days of continuous wind sung through the winding stairs
        when no one rose but the snow,
        when no one looked down but the hawk
        on the wind-tossed waves of pine,
To the weekend stampede, every step with a foot on it
        like the line before a casket
        waiting to take a last look—
And every photo taken on top looks at us,
And graffiti carved everywhere hands could reach considers us,
And the recording never made of all the words spoken on top
        listens to us,
And the movie never made of dismantling the tower dismantles us,
And the lifetime of the ever-changing shadows of the tower
        overshadows us all.

I think I'll climb into the sky
          and look from the lookout awhile.
My feet should be able to find where each step was
          and just where to turn to go up the next flight.
My eyes should be ready by now
          to see what the view has to show.
I want to watch a few centuries go by,
          houses growing closer one by one,
Each in its place replaced by buildings
          replaced in their place by skyscrapers,
And the view from the skyscraper risen from this spot,
          and the proud who scorn elevator
          for stairs,
And the crowds no less mysterious
          yet no less terrifying
          than those in the city I always return to
          wondering if I will always return.
And not till the poet stands where the skyscraper stood
And looking up points out the view
Will I be ready to climb down the invisible stairs of the air
          to be put in his mouth and swallowed
          and called with a whisper—
          *Mescaline.*

# Staff

I have worn smooth with the grip of my hand
      branches found by the trail,
Caught by my eye and lifted,
Thrown in the air and caught by my hand and tested—
      if it's not too long,
      if it's not too short,
      if it feels just right,
I say to myself—"This is my staff!"
      and thump the ground with its end.

Carry me far! Take me where I must go!
Miles away from miles away from every road,
      every house, every human voice
      or voice of machine,
Through woods I love,
Past lakes where no one is,
Beyond where the footpath ends,
      up where the mountains glow
      and the sky has never been breathed!

And should I again among crutches and canes
      unbrellas and books under arms
Walk in the skyscraper's shadow,
It will be with my staff,
It will be in clothes smelling of campfires
      and moss,
And if myriad strangers stare
      curious, suspicious, indignant,
I'll grip my staff tight as I pass
      and let wilderness speak through my mouth
How the feel of this staff
      puts me in touch with the Gods,

Transports me back through the eras,
To the epochs of staff-bearing men,
To the heritage of this wand
          of power and prophecy.

Isn't the only way to write
          with a pencil this size?
For words to be so large
          you must get out your compass,
And the only way to write mountain
          is to climb to the top?

Numberless possible staffs
          wait on the forest floor,
Or fallen from high trees
          caught in their lower branches,
Or resting against a stump
          as if someone left them there.

My walking stick urges me on,
          takes my hand like a friend,
Comforts me, steadies me
          over rough terrain,
Beyond where it's ever been mapped,
Where no human ever set foot,
Following the voice of the stream
          up where the mountains glow
          and the sky has never been breathed!

# Enskyment

Imagine being buried in air,
        in the light blue earth of the sky,
Slowly lowered into thin atmospheres
        on pulleys of evaporation
While shovels of clouds shovel clouds over you
        and you hear far away
The last spadefuls of steeples and fireworks
        and clapping and laughter
And birdsong and forests and mountains
        all scooped on your immense grave of sky!

Imagine those heavenly maggots:
        lost kites, lost balloons,
Seeds we make wishes on,
        butterflies, fireflies,
Wingspreads of vultures,
        and all the nibbling stars.
And branches of trees really roots and roothairs?
        And rainbows really the tunnels of moles?
And earthworms peeping from their holes
        really birdbeaks probing the earth?

What exquisite decay!
All the warmth the sun gives as it melts you!
All those tons of cirrus, stratus, cumulonimbus!
        Skyquakes of lightning!
Your flesh unpetalling in downpours!
Your body become all sunset and ozone,
        delicate rumbles of vanishing thunder!
Till the aroma of sky after rain
        and earth after rain
Is all that's left of your corpse!

# First Drink from a Stream

Into the map feet-first floating downward
I descend toward the first stream I shall drink from
To stand one foot on each bank
With water rushing beneath me.

Before dipping hands brought together
I would whet my thirst with knowing
How many lips searching for lips
Had to come this far for a kiss.

And purer than water is pure,
And cooler than water is cool,
Is the flow of this liquid imagining
Down my esophagus.

Beyond the postures of all the ages
Of animals bending to sip, I kneel,
Lifting in cupped hands
What began and will always begin
From clouds down mountains
Rushing before me and after me
Equal infinities, the living song
Old as water is old
And older than the first boy
Who could suck his own cock
And cupping balls drink from himself
The freshness.

And swallowing I would be quenched
Knowing how little of all the water
That ever feels its way
Through the bed of this stream

Is needed to slake my thirst.
And knowing no name for this stream
I will call it after myself,
As sometimes in my quietest time
I whisper my name to myself
Looking up where I came from
Curious what cupped hands dip from the sky
For one handful of my voice.

# REWORKING WORK

# Rebecca Falls Mescaline Epiphany

We wish that beneficent beings from Outer Space
        would land on earth and bring us the Vision we need
        to save us from destroying the world.
We wish a spaceship would come from Outer Space
        and transport us to its planet's Utopia
        where creatures exactly like us but enlightened
        or creatures very different from us but enlightened
            exist.
We wonder if some of the people we know
        aren't possibly from Outer Space,
Or complete strangers of unearthly beauty
        or great tender geniuses of love,
            poetry, music, dance, art—
        are they not emissaries from "out there"?
We wonder if possibly we are
        Outer Space Reconnaissance Consciousnesses
        programmed not to awake till now,
Cosmic Reconnaissance Renaissance Consciousnesses
        programmed not to awake till now.
What is my Mission on this Planet?
What am I here for? What am I here for?
Ding! Ding! Ding! Ding! Ding!
Suddenly we realize WE ARE FROM OUTER SPACE!
        WE ARE CREATURES FROM OUTER SPACE!
        EARTH IS OUR PLANET IN OUTER SPACE!
We don't have to go in a spaceship from Earth to the moon
        and take Mescaline and look back at our Earth
            or walk in space after smoking
            millions of joints
        to realize we're in Outer Space!
We are just as much in Outer Space
        wherever we are on this Planet
            as we'd be on our moon

or any moon in our solar system
        or any solar system in this galaxy
    or any galaxy in this universe
        or any universe in the pastpresentfuture!
We are as much creatures from Outer Space
        as lifeforms anywhere in this galaxy
            or any galaxy!
There's nowhere in the Universe
        that is more in Outer Space
        than we are!
We live *in* the Universe!
It's not "out there."
It's not just something we see in movies
        to eerie music.
We don't have to read science fiction
        to make love voluptuous cricketsinging nights
            under all the stars.
Thank you Mescaline and Marijuana for helping us perceive
        the mystical miraculousness of every day and every second
        and all living forms of life and every climate
        and geology, the seasons, the natures of
            seeing, hearing, smelling, tasting, touching,
            sleeping, dreaming, waking, laughing, loving,
            and the transformation of death!
Each of us should be as much an apparition as Bigfoot
        or LochNess Monster!
Each of us should be as much an apparition as the Being
        coming down the ramp of the spaceship
            from "out there."
How dear this Earth becomes then!
How sacred every wild place and creature
        that remains!
How insidious and lamentable the vast factory's pollution
        and overpopulation disaster more disastrous
            than all the dead in every human war!
How clear it becomes to us then
        that no one should have to be a slave!

That everyone should be a creative genius of tender love
      and loving creator of music or poetry,
         painting or dance,
      endless continued gentle passionate creations
         of human mind!
Behold the lilies, they neither spin nor sew!
Think of the whales! They don't punch timeclocks!
      They don't need Christ or Buddha
         to be enlightened.
Everyone's life should be devoted to enlightenment!
Everyone should be free to receive Visions of Mescaline
      in absolute wilderness solitude!
Ah, I feel the key, for me, to perceiving, entertaining,
      and embodying Infinite Space and Eternal Time's
         Ultimate Implications are to be found
      in the deepest solitude I can find
         in the non-human Manifestation of Cosmos
      in that realm called Wilderness Reality.
What does Contemporary Poetry Scene in America
      have to do with this?
Do I live in America? Is it 1984?
Do people who are dead continue to argue
      whether there is life after death?
This *is* Heaven!
I don't have to die
      to be Immortal!
I don't have to die
      to be in Eternity!
To feel in this flash of existence
      in the Antler form
      the unending Amaze!
O Poets are Emissaries from Outer Space
      descending their spaceship ramps
      and their visionary message to Earth
         shall be heard around the world!

## Written After Learning
## Slaves in Ancient Greece and Rome
## Had 115 Holidays a Year

Instead of creating better murder weapons
        to "protect" ourselves,
Better create loving boys and girls
        who become loving women and men.
Instead of a higher standard of living
        why not a higher standard of loving?
Why not a higher standard
        of getting high?
No more brainwashed robotzombies!
No more socialization lobotomies!

Thoreau could live a whole year
        on money from working 6 weeks.
We canned ourselves in concentrationcamps
        called cities
And in buildings and rooms where we work.
We have become hermetically sealed containers.
The can of today is the wilderness that was.
The can-to-be is the wilderness that is.

As Oscar Wilde said: "Work is the curse
        of the drinking man."
As Stan Jones said: "It's not what the machine makes,
        but what the machine makes you."
As Virgil said: *Deus nobis haec otia fecit:*
        "A god has granted us this idleness."
As Lessing said: "Let us be lazy in everything
        except in loving and drinking,
        except in being lazy."

Should cans stop being made?
Should all factories immediately close down?
What solution do you provide? If everyone's a poet
            and no one works, how do we survive?
The way St. Theresa survived on Light?
Love becomes a full-time job?
But where do we get the money
            to pay people not to work?

Slaves in Ancient Greece and Rome
            had 115 holidays a year!
Hey, wait a minute, that makes us
            more slaves than them!

# The Way I Figure It

The way I figure it
No one should be a slave.
Everyone should be free.
When I think of my own life
      I think Wow,
Already I've worked over five years
      in factories!
For working that long I deserve
      the rest of my life
      to be a paid vacation.
Then I start thinking of my mother
      and brother and sister
      and friends
Chained to jobs they have to put up with,
Yet my father being dead is free from all that,
But when I think how he only got
      a three week vacation every year,
Or how the 12-hour day 6-day workweek for pittance
      was once taken for granted,
When people got a one-week vacation
      in their 20s or 30s
Or a two-week vacation
      in their 40s or 50s . . .
I've got to make up for them by golly!
Why, every day a person works in a factory
I figure that gives them a year's vacation,
So boy oh boy, I gotta lotta vacations
      to live in a single life!
Maybe I'll give a few out to you
      my friends and readers.
Maybe if we all realize we should be
      all making up for the wasted lives

(So many now in the history of humans
          each of us would have to live a million lives
          to make up for all their lost vacations)
We can get back in touch with the time
          we were less like ants
And more like eagles soaring
          over the wilderness realms of the earth.

## For the Six Children Brutally Murdered by Their Father, My Cousin's Child Dead by Disease, and Walt Cieszynski Killed in Carcrash

When Walt died I remember thinking now I have to write
      the poems he won't be around to write,
Now I have to make up for all the poems
      never written.
I have to live the ecstasies the children
      murdered by their fathers
      or dying from disease
      will never feel,
The poems they would've lived or written.
Then I think of the sick thoughts, the brutal ways of living
      perpetrated on so many children.
The very fact children must spend so much time in school
      or adults in offices and factories
      is an atrocity in itself.
Anyone who has to make a living to live,
Who has to work a slavejob all their life,
      haven't they been brutally murdered?
Don't I have to make up for all their life
      never lived?
Experience all the wilderness they never will?
Smoke all the grass I can for their lack of imbibing
      that sacred high,
Sex all the joys I can for those who never have
      or will?

Oh, I have to make up for all the wasted and cutshort lives,
      all the lost opportunities!
To think of my thirty-one years I've only had three autumns
      with the total of every day free
      to savor the changes of foliage and weather
      in wilderness on this planet!

There's so much to learn, so much to experience,
There's not time in a hundred lifetimes to do it all.
But the only way to start is to be free
                and in that freedom to be free
To make up for all the lives cut short
                by murder or disease or carcrash
Or a livelihood that's a deathlihood
                to the soul and the earth.

# Factories Are Boxcars Full of Jews

The multiplication of cells of urban hives,
Cramming the human spirit into them
        with truncheons of work ethic.
Children molested by 18,000 murders
        and a million commercials
        seen on TV by age 18,
Their fathers job fodder of cannibal consumerism,
Their mothers soap opera gameshow junkies.
Cigarets and their advertisements.
Poisonfood and their advertisements.
All the tools of murder and pollution
        created by Factories—
What difference between this and Hitler elated
        with unfolding blueprint of gaschambers?
Once more the massacre of millions.
Once more mass graves there isn't time to bury.
Once more the words "atrocity" and "genocide"
        find their proper (undeniable) identification.
Every large city could at any moment become
        an Auschwitz of nuclear incineration.

Were those who worked toward the murder
        of 6 million Jews
Worse than those who work toward the murder
        of all human life?
Christ's crucifixion only lasted three hours.
Most workers are crucified their whole lives
Their souls impaled by spikes
        from which their useless bodies
        and undiscovered continents of epiphany hang.
What future is there for Utopia
When most humans spend most of their lives

Working jobs they hate, working jobs
        that directly or indirectly
        contribute to Planet Death?
What difference between this and the Nazis
        pumping Zyklon B into gaschambers?
What the Nazis did to the Jews
        Factories are doing to the Earth.

Like volcanoes that never stop erupting,
Each continually overflowing its own kind of lava
Inundating us—here a volcano of cans,
        here a volcano of guns,
        here a volcano of cars,
        here a volcano of bombs,
Or like huge galleys, triremes,
        and each slave at his oar,
Never able to come topside,
Following the beat of the drum,
        feeling the bite of the lash,
Some thinking death is better
        than life like this,
Some wishing they'd never been born.

# Zero-Hour Day Zero-Day Workweek

Are the executives of oil steel aluminum plastic
       military industrial capitalism
To be looked up to as Great Men and Women to be held
       as fitting examples of enlightened human beings?
Or are they miserable failures of greed who betray the Earth
       and the promise of America?
Is who invented napalm to be honored?
Is who invented nervegas to be honored?
Slavery did not end. Almost everyone enslaved
       to earthdeath accomplice jobs.
A new Emancipation Proclamation is needed.
Liberation from an 8-hour day 5-day workweek
       to a 5-hour day 1-day workweek
       getting paid the same amount.
Or how about a 12-hour day 7-day playweek?
Or maybe keep only the least harmful factories
       and everyone has to factory once for a year,
       the rest of their life free to learn and create,
       travel to wilds and other lands, like Huxley's *Island*?

We think working 8 hours a day
       a great advance over the time
       when workers, even children,
       worked 14 hours a day
       for lousy wages and conditions.
It *is* better, but 8 hours a day
       is still too long!
Our lives should be free, a continual vacation.
Anyone who had to work all their life
       and had a two-week vacation every year
       has been robbed.

Anyone who had to work six months a year
      and had a six-month vacation
      has been robbed.
Anyone who had to work one day a year
      and had a 364-day vacation
      has been robbed.
Only Total Vacation will do.


Expand Wilderness, Reduce Population, Reduce Production!
Anyone who says it can't be done is performing what I call
      "The Ghost Dance in Reverse."
We can shape the Image of Man we desire!
We can shape the Image of Boy we desire!
We can shape the Image of Girls and Women and America
      and World Peace and Wilderness VisionQuest Enlightenment
      we desire!
A 12-hour day 6-day workweek
      becomes a 10-hour day 6-day workweek
      becomes an 8-hour day 5-day workweek
      becomes a 6-hour day 4-day workweek
      becomes a 4-hour day 2-day workweek
      becomes a 1-hour day 1-day workweek
      becomes a 0-hour day 0-day workweek!


People should be paid not to work!
People should be paid to play!
People should lie in hammocks
      and sip lemonade all day!
Most people are too busy working or resting from work
      to work on their own mindgrowth poet-ential.
"But," my mother asks, "what about workers who *like*
      their jobs—happy they receive so much money
      to buy all the amazing things factories make
      not to mention the benefits they get
      for medical protection and old age?"
It's not religion that's the opium of the people, but *work*,

Work is the opium of the people. O Workers of the World,
        stop working!
Think of the whales, more intelligent than Einstein or Bach,
        who never have to work a fucking second
        of their incredible life!

# Workaholics Anonymous

The notion the main purpose of life is to work
    is a worse malady than alcoholism.
We could have an economy based on play
      where the purpose of life is geared
         more to play/ecstasy/meditation
    than workbeast deathlihood.
America is a Workaholic!
Antler invents Workaholics Anonymous
    where workaholics go
      to be talked out of working
    and where workers laid off or unemployed
      go to memorize my "Factory" poem
    and philosophize in pastoral settings
    about Work's place in Life.
Were people meant to do backbreaking
    minddeadening work their whole lives?
It's time to rework our notions of work.
It's time to commute the sentence
    of everyone sentenced to commute.
It's time to take back the time taken from us
    and have the time of our lives.
The purpose of life is not to work meaningless jobs
    that destroy the Earth.
Re-educate people to see
    the main purpose of existence
      is creative play and ecstasy
    and work should play
      a minor part.
Restore semblance of balance
    between work and play
      from whose harmony more lives
    will be realized.

Aren't human beings actually inferior
    to plants and animals who have no slaves,
        factories, wars, but are content
    simply to *be*?

Do Sequoias need to take courses in business administration?
Do Blue Whales need a stock exchange or Wall Street?
When Sequoias grow up do they have to get a job
    and get only a one-week vacation every year?
Do Blue Whales have to fulfill their military obligation?
Do Birds have to read books to learn how to migrate
    or carry factory-made compasses to guide them?
Must Robins spin treadmills to earn metal discs
    to purchase their worms?
Do Sequoias have to work all their lives in factories
    to pay off the mortgage on their homes?
Are Blue Whales fashion-conscious?
Do Sequoias erect statues of dead Sequoias they think were great
    so future Sequoias can contemplate them?
And when a Sequoia tree dies it stands a thousand years
    before it falls and when it falls
        it takes a thousand years
        before it rots away.
Rather than megalomaniacs of megalopolis,
    quiescent Sequoias sequestering.
Rather than machinations of mechanization,
    the actualization of ecstasy.
Rather than a species becomes extinct every second,
    a factory becomes extinct every second.
Rather than factory, fuckery!
Isness rather than Bizness.
Do Eagles have little green slips of paper
    they have to sweat in sweatshops to get
        so they can buy the food they need
    and pay rent on their eyries
        and shop for feathers to keep warm?

No matter how cheap you make shoes
              deer will go barefoot.

Workers angry they're out of work. Ha!
What about all those working who are *out of play*!
As if total freedom wasn't the lifework of the creative spirit!
Factoryslaves should complain
              they're out of play—
They need freedom more than someone out of work
              needs a job.
Joblessness? Ha! What about Playlessness?
If there is a work force
              why not a play force?
Play ethic vs. work ethic.
Playaholic vs. workaholic.
People think it's a disgrace not to work,
              that one is being irresponsible,
But actually it's those working ecocide jobs
              who are most irresponsibly irresponsible.
The problem is not that the economy is faltering
              but that freedom is faltering.
Rather than create more jobs
              why not create more freedom?
The more we work the less we're free!
We're brainwashed to believe
              there's something called an Economy
              and that when you grow up
You have to get a job and work
              most of the waking hours of your life
              to get those little green slips of paper.

The trouble with America is
              not that it's out of work
              but that it's out of Poetry.
Writing Poetry is a 48-hour-a-day job.

**125**

The Poet is never unemployed or laid off,
　　　gets no vacations,
　　　　　must always be on call
　　　to deliver the God from his mouth.
Parents should want their children to be poets
　　　more than priests, lawyers, bankers, executives.
Put America back to Work?
Put America back to Play!
Put America back to Poetry!
ReWilderness America!
To accuse me of being a sluggard
　　　is an insult to slugs!
No grub is a moneygrubber!
"You're making the workers feel bad about their jobs."
　　　Right!
"You're making them feel like zombies."
　　　Right!
In San Francisco 400 apply for hotel bellhop job
　　　that pays $4.97 per hour.
Why not 400 apply for job as Poet?
Blacks want 40 trillion dollars reparations
　　　for all the unpaid work
　　　　　their ancestors did as slaves.
The Polish Parliament overwhelmingly approves
　　　a tough "social parasites" law
　　　　　authorizing forced labor and jail terms
　　　for those believed to be avoiding work. ⸙
Poles between 18 and 45 out of work three months
　　　must register with the state.
Those deemed evading work
　　　for "socially unjustified reasons"
　　　　　are forced to work two months
　　　"for public purposes"
　　　　　and risk two-year jail terms
　　　and confiscation of apartments.
As Carl Sandburg said: "Freedom is everyone's job,
　　　everyone is freedom's job."

As Diane di Prima said: "If what you want is jobs for everyone
      you are still the enemy."
As St. Pol-Roux had a sign on his door as he slept
      which said: "Do not disturb,
          Poet at work."

## Dream Job Offer

Demonstrate comfort of fancy bedroom set
By sleeping in department store display window
       facing busy downtown street.
Punch in, put on your pj's,
       get into bed
       and go to sleep.
Shoppers walk by,
       gawk and talk.
8 hours later alarm tingalings
       it's upping time. Return home
       to write down your dreams.
Make money while you sleep!
Only those who enjoy sleeping need apply.
No bedwetters, wetdreamers, sleeptalkers,
       sleepwalkers, teethgrinders,
       buzz-saw snorers, or those who
       wake up in a cold sweat screaming
       will be hired.
Must have experience, Degree in Sleepology
       required.

## Why No "Poet Wanted" in Want Ad Column

Those who regard it an affront you write poems
        and aren't working—
As if writing poems and being a poet were not valid work
        in our society,
As if Poetry has no value,
Especially when you write
        "Factories Are Boxcars Full of Jews,"
Especially when you invoke a marijuana blowjob religion,
Especially when you place Solitude Wilderness Vision Quest
        above all the Works of Man.
They want you to get a job you don't like
        and have to be working full-time
        so you can't write anymore.
They want you to confess
        your poetry is full of shit.
Somehow your writing
        threatens them.
Besides, Christ already said it all—
So don't bother trying to say
        something new that's true.
What are the words of a mere mortal
        next to the Son of God's?

# For the Recognition of the Role of the Poet in Society

James Dickey once said poets inspired by Ginsberg or Bly
    would be better off to society
    employed as garbage collectors.
What an insult, I thought, till I learned
Garbage collectors in California make $25,000 a year!
And a poet, after cost of paper, pencils, pens,
    envelopes, stamps, xeroxing,
On the average makes minus $1000 a year.
But Poetry is great, greater than most poets realize.
Enough poets have scrawled "Dead Poet" on their t-shirts
    and jumped off the Golden Gate Bridge.
As there is the expression "to put someone to death,"
    Poetry's purpose is "to put someone to life."
What kind of society can you expect
    where poets make less than garbage collectors?
Wouldn't that make poetry less than garbage?
Wouldn't that make parents want their children
    to grow up to be garbage collectors
    rather than poets?
Poets are more important than presidents.
Poets are more important than executives.
Poets are more important
    than even most poets realize.

## "Your Poetry's No Good Because It Tries to Convey a Message"

Tell it to Jews hanging from meathooks,
Tell it to Wilfred Owen's exploded face,
Tell it to James Wright's cancerous cut-out tongue,
Tell it to Victor Jara's hands chopped off
        in Santiago Stadium,
Tell it to all the ears, breasts, cocks and balls
        cut off in every war,
Tell it to all the beautiful eyes
        gouged out in every war,
Tell it to the pyramid of human skulls
        that never stops growing,
Tell it to the decapitated head held up
        to gape twitching corpse jeering crowd,
Tell it to the fact we're all in Auschwitz because
        any second every city can become Holocaust,
Tell it to Hetch Hetchy, tell it to Glen Canyon,
        tell it to Wounded Knee and the Buffalo,
Tell it to the aluminum fibres in your brain
        and the cancer in your food and water
        which will eventually kill you,
Tell it to 100 trillion cigarets a year,
Tell it to 100 billion spent on war every minute,
Tell it to Johnny Got His Gun,
Tell it to the ashes of Neruda's library,
Tell it to 52 million children under 15
        working in factories in Southeast Asia,
Tell it to more people born in 2984
        than all the people ever born,
Tell it to the annihilated White Pine dominions
        of Wisconsin,
Tell it to the Sequoias still standing
        who were alive one thousand years
        before the Bible was written,

Tell it to all the unexperienced homosexual joy
          since Christianity came into power,
Tell it to the $100,000 it cost to kill
          each soldier in World War II,
Tell it to Henry Ford's factory in France
          that made tanks for the Third Reich,
Tell it to the sunrise, tell it to the rainbow,
          tell it to the flower made love to by the bee,
Tell it to the waterfall that never stops telling,
Tell it to the combers that never cease crashing,
Tell it to the reflection of stars
          in the rain-filled blackbear track,
Tell it to the canyons that echo
          the canyons that echo,
Tell it to birdsong, whalesong, wolfsong, cricketsong,
Tell it to the clouds as they float overhead,
          yell it to the lightning, bell it to the thunder,
          well it to the pouring rain, spell it
              on kindergarten blackboard,
          knell it to firefly cemetery dusk,
Tell it to tombstones who have forgotten their names,
Tell it to the shadow of your breathcloud
          on a winter day,
Tell it to mother harp seals
          while their babies are skinned alive,
Tell it to the naked black youth being hung
          by white lynchmob while they point and laugh,
Tell it to the geniuses who invent better and better
          methods of mass murder,
Tell it to the stockpiles of suicide pills
          to be dispensed in the event of apocalypse,
Tell it to the fact more women raped in America every year
          than poetry books sold every year,
Tell it to the statistics of ecocide, genocide, suicide,
Tell it to Kennedy's brainfragments
          quivering on the Dallas street,

Tell it to Sylvia Plath's head in the oven,
Tell it to Lorca while the soldier fires
          two bullets up his ass.

# Truncheons of Work-Ethic Bludgeoning

Why is a soaring eagle
    such an inspiring sight?
Because we'd like to be like that,
Effortlessly soaring above it all,
Able to glide on the wind all day
    without even moving our wings.
Yet how many of the five billion humans
    live lives as magnificent
    as a soaring eagle?
Who ever thinks of a soaring ant
    or a soaring sheep?

Every 8 hours more babies born
    than U.S. soldiers killed
    in every war America fought.
800,000 people per square mile
    in some parts of Hong Kong.
More people in the San Francisco Bay Area
    than the total population of North America
    in 1776.
At the current growth rate in 2000 years
    everything in the visible universe
    will be converted to people
    and the ball of people
Will be expanding
    with the speed
    of light.

500 million tons of poison
    belch from smokestacks every year.
20,000 wild lakes in Ontario
    killed by acid rain by 2000.

3000 square miles of Amazon rainforest
       cut down each month.
Over half the world's trees cut down since 1950.
At the present growth rate in the use
       of the ten most-used minerals
       we will mine the equivalent of
       the Earth's weight in 300 years.
Souls strip-mined and clear-cut by work-ethic!
It's because we're so patriotic toward our factories
       we have to have enough bombs to blow up the Earth
       a hundred times.
It's because it's easier to support our family
       via factory than poetry
       we're never more than 20 minutes
       from the end of the world.
It's because the workers don't want
       their factories to close down
       we have enough plutonium to kill
       everyone 10 times.
It's because the workers don't want
       to lose their jobs
       they have lost their freedom.
It's because it's thought satisfactory for most of us
       to spend most of the waking hours of our lives
       in a factory
Christianity can get people to believe
Paradise and Immortality
       come only after we die—
Rather than now.

But Christ wasn't kidding when he urged us consider
       the lilies who neither spin nor sew
       yet each is clothed in raiment finer
       than Solomon in all his factories.
Heaven is now. We can live forever NOW!
To an Eagle a single second in a cage is intolerable.

**135**

A single adult Grizzly needs a home-range of 64,000 acres.
As for the benefits factories confer—
Tell it to Ishi on the L.A. Freeway during rush hour,
Tell it to Black Elk on Times Square at midnight
        on New Year's Eve,
Tell it to the Blue Whales and Redwoods
        murdered by harpoons and buzz-saws,
Tell it to the shadowgraphs in Hiroshima,
Tell it to the poets on Skid Row.

## Winter Night Can Plant Return

Ten years after completing *Factory*
One snowy cold January night I return
        to my old alma mater—
Walk north along railroad tracks
        from Riverside Park to Estabrook Park,
Cutting across the snowy parkscape
        looking up at the Channel 6 Tower,
Over to the wooded slopes of the Milwaukee River
        and along the snowy trail,
Smelling the factory before actually seeing it,
        the acrid chemical taint,
Hearing the factory before actually seeing it,
        the weird metallic buzz,
Finally reaching where more rail tracks
        cross the river on an old wooden trestle,
Glimpsing through tree-branches at the slope's crest
        across the river through tree-branches
        beyond the far slope,
The gigantic can plant, all windows lit,
        thousandfold machineroar humming.
About to cross over
        I see a light flash from behind me
        and hear a train approach.
Backing into the brush, hiding behind an oak
        I spy the slow advance.
An old locomotive rumbles across,
        the bridge groans under its weight,
        the engineer peering ahead through falling snow,
The snow-hung trees illuminated, the swirls
        of snowgusts illuminated, then darkened
        as the lightbeam passes,

The darkened boxcars passing through falling snow,
     swaying gently side to side,
Ten boxcars full of coils of aluminum
     to be turned into millions of cans.
In the distance near the barbed-wire gate
     at the factory's rear
     a man swinging a lantern.
After uncoupling its load inside
     and switching tracks
       the engine returns alone.
After it's gone and its decrescendoing rumble is gone
     I cautiously cross the bridge
Pausing a moment halfway, gazing upstream—
     the snow-covered ice, the tree-lined
     dark park riverbanks, the wild night river scene
      juxtaposed to Industry's Monument,
Nearer yet I approach you O Factory
     from which *Factory* originated!
Unsuspecting giant, blizzard-engulfed,
     closer, closer—inside through your windows
     once more I see the workers and the machines.
Funny, I could be a saboteur with a bomb,
     or a spy or assassin.
Then I remember I already revealed
     the top secret in *Factory*,
     already blew up all factories with poetry.
This must be a deathbed mirage,
This trembling earth, this noise, these fumes,
     the huge architecture is a dream.
Perhaps I lived here 5000 years ago
     and time-warped into the future
     to glimpse what was in store.
Perhaps my spaceship landed from another planet
     and I emerged onto this scene.
Perhaps I died in the Wilderness and my spirit
     returned here for some reason.

Secret rendezvous, secret rendezvous,
How could I have known how powerful you'd be to me?
The swirling snow, the intense cold, long after midnight,
          no one else here,
No one on Earth knows I'm here
Standing smoking ceremonial smoke
          on the deep snow tree-lined bluff,
              looking over at and into Continental Can,
                  musing and being mused by these thoughts.
Why didn't the owners answer my letter
Requesting to give a performance of *Factory*
          to the workers in the plant
              when I sent them a complimentary copy?
Ten years after completing it I return
          to find a sprawling two-story addition
          plus another vast parking lot.
What good did my poem do after all?
The Factory I made disappear ten years ago
          is twice as big!
Yet the very fact I stand here
          smoking superb marijuana contemplation
          confronting the actual monster
              is a victory, as much a coup
          as Sioux brave touching his enemy
          and able to escape unharmed—
Only this "enemy" is working so hard
          it doesn't even know I'm here. . . .
Snow covers my boots, icicles hang from my beard
          before I realize how long I've been standing
              motionless in the blizzard
              looking in.
And then, retreating, beginning my long hike home,
          stopping every so often to look back,
              to see the receding vision
Till the canplant is lost from view,
Till only the noise and smell and trembling
          pervade the plummeting rivercrest trail—

**139**

The epiphany, earthshaking
        as the earthshaking from factoryroar,
That it was when the locomotive vanished
        and its big noise vanished
        that the reality of the continuing noise
            and earthquake tremble from canfactory
        rushed in on me,
Realization the ground-vibrating machineroar
        radiates outward in every direction
Like an earthquake that never stops.
How far out does that quake tremble?
What effect those tremors
        on our flesh, bones, brains?
As in diagrams projecting the impact
        of a nuclear bomb on a city
We should draw concentric circles from each factory
        to show the intensity, the reality
Each factory is a ground zero exploding
        its noise, products, pollution
            in every direction,
The same as a bomb exploding
        but continuously for decades
            and each of us blown up
        our whole life.

# CATCHING
# THE SUNRISE

## Raising My Hand

One of the first things we learn in school is
            if we know the answer to a question
We must raise our hand and be called on
            before we can speak.
How strange it seemed to me then,
            raising my hand to be called on,
How at first I just blurted out,
            but that was not permitted.

How often I knew the answer
And the teacher (knowing I knew)
Called on others I knew (and she knew)
            had it wrong!
How I'd stretch my arm
            as if it would break free
            and shoot through the roof
            like a rocket!
How I'd wave and groan and sigh,
Even hold up my aching arm
            with my other hand
Begging to be called on,
Please, *me*, I know the answer!
Almost leaping from my seat
            hoping to hear my name.

Twenty-nine now, alone in the wilds,
Seated on some rocky outcrop
            under all the stars,
I find myself raising my hand
            as I did in first grade

Mimicking the excitement
        and expectancy felt then.
No one calls on me
        but the wind.

# What the God Says Through Me

You won't hear my poems at the poetry reading.
You won't hear my poems over the radio.
If you want what the God says through me
Come alone with me into Quetico
        and we'll canoe across lake after lake
        where there are no roads or houses
To a perfect lake with a perfect island
Where you and I will pitch our camp
        and catch fish for twilight supper.

Sitting around the fire at night
Ask me to read something I wrote
For this is the place to hear me,
More stars overhead than you ever saw,
        no other light in the woods for miles,
        no other sound but the loon
And the night wilderness smells of September.
This is the place to hear my voice
        if you want what the God says through me.

## This Is the Poet Pipe

This is the Poet Pipe!
This is the Pipe of Poetry!
I offer it to be smoked
        by all the poets I love.
I offer the best grass in the world
        for the sacred ceremony.
We will pass the pipe in a circle
        for centuries on centuries.
The seasons shall come and go
        as we smoke ourselves into being.
We will smoke the marijuana that grows
        from the graves of our ancestors.
Their Immortality
        shall make us high.

## Put This in Your Pipe and Smoke It!

If the solar system were five miles long
        the sun would be a three-foot sphere
            and the earth a pea a footballfield away!
If the Milky Way were ten miles long
        the solar system would be the size of a pinhead
            and the sun a millionth of an inch!
If the sun were the dot over an "i"
        the nearest star would be the dot over an "i"
            24 miles away!
A million earths could easily fit in our sun
        yet some stars are so big
            six billion suns our size
                could easily fit inside!

The size of my winking eye compared to the sun!

# Alan Watts Dying in His Sleep Elegy

"What will it be like to go to sleep and never wake up?
It makes me inevitably think of my birth, of waking up
after having never gone to sleep!"

                                        —*Beyond Theology* by Alan Watts

It was the new grass and Jeff couldn't wait.
I was just lighting a match when Jim and Carol came in the door
And the telephone rang with my mother telling me
           the newspaper said
Alan Watts died in his sleep.

After the first joint I sat in my antique dentist chair
           and taking the paddle I used in Quetico
                 I paddled the air
           till I was in my canoe once more
                 in the middle of Solitude Lake.
After the second joint Jim whispered
           you can go so far down in Mammoth Cave
                 above the ceiling an underground river flows
           so big you can take boat trips on it
                 and above the ceiling above the river
           lies an even more immense room of the cave,
And then Carol whispered a day's drive from Milwaukee
           are caves with sixty-foot underground waterfalls,
                 and the way she told it
           we were there.
After the third joint Jeff and I became young animals
           wrestling and growling and biting each other
                 to Beethoven mandolins
Till Jim appeared with a tub of hot water to soak our feet in
           while conducting the Vienna Choirboys

accompanied by harp and the fourth joint
laughing at the growing pool on the rug
Till Carol and I lugged the leaky tub to the porch
and raced barefoot around the November block
till back on the stoop, pants rolled to knees,
we poured warm water over numb feet
watching it waterfall down the steps
and the rising steam
And before she knew it I'd locked her out
and when she knocked
the door opened a crack grinning
"Who are you and what do you want?"
And after letting her in to Kodaly's songs for girls' chorus
I crawled toward my writing room
gibbering like a thirst-crazed man
And crawling back with another joint
of the best grass since I smoked wilderness
we smoked it
And then Chopin made me take the mirror shaped like a tombstone
and walk toward Jim with it in front of my face
so he saw his own face coming toward him
and from behind his closed lips my voice—
"How can I speak when I don't open my mouth?"
And then sitting down facing Jeff with his face
I said—"What's your name? Can we be friends?"
And turning the mirror around on my lap
I looked in my own face with surprise,
gentleness, infatuation, lust,
the slow blossoming of my smile,
And watching myself laugh
I wished we all had mirrors on our laps
and could have conversations with each other
while watching ourselves speak,
And then Jeff put on Milhaud's "Scaramouche"
and sitting facing each other
balancing our feet

we took turns dancing the beat
      on each other's soles
passing back and forth laughs we hadn't laughed
      since wilderness smoked us,
And after the sixth wilderness I floated
      the beaverskull from Quetico in candlelight
      toward Carol's face
And accompanied by Jeff and Jim's shouts of "Popcorn! Popcorn!"
      I told Carol I believe each of us is living right now
      on millions of planets
      because if I were God I'd have made it that way,
And then I created popcorn
      with just enough butter
      and we washed it down with cold slugs of beer
And after the seventh day of creation
      Jeff brought in ten concert grands
      playing the William Tell Overture
And I stood on my head till I no longer could
Then danced with the mirror
      whirling in circles at top speed
      till my reflection and I collapsed
      in epilepsies of laughter
      and sprawled exhaustion my heart
      pounding harder than ever
      gazing up at the ceiling still spinning
      as the lights clicked on and off on and off
      on and off on and off on and off . . .

Alan Watts—*you'll never know you died.*

                                    November 17, 1973

# The Hereafter of Laughter

Are all my laughs immortal?
        my babychortle?
        my laughs in the womb?
My childhood and boyhood
        growing laugh?
My glut of mirth?
My epitome of buffooneries?
My bearded and well-grained laugh?
Do they still exist?
Will I return to them
        or they to me?
Will I reunion with my past laughs
        after I die?
The old man praying on his deathbed
        to be united with his boyhood laugh?
The boy waking up laughing from his dream
        to silence and darkness?
Will all my most heartfelt laughs
        greet me into heaven?

# The Earth's Business

The Earth's business is
           Corpses Incorporated
And it uses maggots
           for money.

# Deathrattles

Yes or No? If there is life after death,
        if there is reincarnation,
Will each of us have so many lives
That all our deathrattles put together
        over Eternity
Take up more time than all the lives
That ever lived on earth
        put together?

# The Rebirth of My Mouth

Now I return to the forgotten way.
I throw away my fork and spoon.
My knife? I will use my mouth
           for killing now.
My teeth are sharp enough.
My jaws are strong enough
           to tear off chunks of living flesh.
I can crush skulls
           with a single bite,
Rip throats, tear guts in a second,
Eat the eyes while they still can see
And the ears while they can still hear.

I began by eating with my fingers.
Then it was time for my hands
           to be tied behind my back,
To bend over the plate and eat like that.
Then it was time to let myself loose
           four-legged in the woods for a summer,
To re-learn how to stalk
           or lie in wait for my prey,
To remember at last
           the best place to bite
           to slaughter my food.
Now I am ready to kiss.
Now I am ready to speak
           of joy and truth
           with my mouth.

# The Darkness Within

One hand on your chest,
One hand on your back—
      the distance between,
Between what can be seen—
      the chest, the back,
And the darkness within,
What you never see, touch of yourself,
      lungs, heart, liver, stomach,
      kidneys, intestines, skeleton.
You will die without holding
      your heart in your hands.
You will die without holding
      your 28 feet of intestines.
No way to hold your own skull
      unless you cut off your head,
      boil off the flesh.
And the darkness within your balls.
All that semen, yet not white
      till it sees the light of day.
And all your blood pulsing inside you
      this instant—is it red
      or black?
Black! Did you think there are lights
      under your skin that illumine
      your insides so your insides
      can see themselves?
It's darker inside your body
      than in a forest at night.
And you think you know yourself!
Why the only way to even begin
      is to vivisectionize yourself.
So what if it hurts.

You have a responsibility to the inquiry
        of human identity's self-discovery
        even if it kills you.
What else is Poetry for?

# Making Love to the Dark

When you have sex in complete darkness
You make love to the dark
        and the dark makes love to you.
You hug and are hugged by the dark.
You kiss and are kissed by the dark.
The night plays with your cock
        with its dark fingers.
The tight asshole of midnight
        breathes your cock in.
The slippery, rippling vagina of night
        invisible, warm and moist
        enfolds your cock.
You are fucking and being fucked
        by the night.
You are sucking and being sucked
        by the night.
You are jacking off and being jacked off
        by the night.
The thought of white semen spurting in darkness
        where it can't be seen
        obsesses you.
O to know what it's like to be blind!
To know what it's like to make love
        for one who cannot see!

## Playing Dead Love

How many of us have forgotten
How we loved pretending to die,
How we spent afternoons ecstatic
Being killed by make-believe bullets
Or in a duel of invisible swords
        stabbed in the heart.
No one could make the sounds of guns and bombs
        better than us.
We were virtuosos of ricochet sounds.
Slave, Guard, Spy, Explorer, Pirate, King—
We were them all in our secret games.
Each of us knew in his own best way
When the imagined foe dealt the mortal blow
        just how to topple
        down snowy hills
Rolling every posture into a tumbled sprawl
        and there, at the bottom
        in that breathless Wow
We'd lay, playing dead the way we loved,
Motionless, watching the drifting sky,
Or eyes closed, feeling the earth spin
Letting ourselves be buried
By softly falling snow
        till we heard our mother
        in the growing dark
        calling us home.

# Pretending to Be Dead

How many boys who loved playing army,
Who loved pretending to be shot
       tumbling down summer hills,
Who loved pretending to be dead
       as their bestfriend checked to make sure,
Or who loved pretending to deliver
       their last-words soliloquy
       wincing in imagined pain
       or lost and dreamy,
Find themselves years later
       trapped on the battlefield
Hearing the voices of enemy soldiers
Searching for corpses to mutilate
       or wounded to torture to death?

What man remembers those idyllic
       boyhood days then
As he lies still as possible
Trying not even to breathe,
       hoping beyond hope
       the enemy will pass him by,
Knowing if he's discovered
       they'll cut off his cock and balls
       and stuff them in his screaming mouth
And then, before cutting off his head,
       disembowel him before his eyes?

Ah, thousands of boys and men
       have met this end,
Millions perhaps by now,
       so many people
       so many wars.

Do they go to a special heaven
          set aside for
          all who die like this?
Restored to the bodies they had,
The memory erased of that insane end
          to the story of their lives?

Do they still get a chance
          to play army with joy
And pretend to be shot
          and pretend to die
After they meet this end?
Do they still get to thrill
          in pretending to be dead
          after they die?
After this hideous inhuman end
          will they laugh and wrestle
          their bestfriend again?

# Bringing Zeus to His Knees

In the drained reflecting pool in the small park
    facing San Francisco City Hall during
    the June 12, 1982 Disarmament Anti-Nuclear Rally
A barechested boy lying on his back, arms behind
    his head, eyes closed,
    sunbasking.
As speaker after speaker gives
    inspiring talk
And the crowd roars and applauds,
    all faces turned toward the stage,
The boy lies there—where last week seagulls floated
    on turquoise ripples.
Does he hear the great pleas for peace?
Or is he dozing?
Perhaps he was listening before
    behind his closed eyes
    his dreamlovegirl or boy appeared
    and glowed and gleamed.
How many loving eyes caress this Vision
    that does not see them?
How many strolling from the rapt crowd
    to rest their ears from the anti-war fervor
    they so much agree with
    and which inspires so many of their poems,
Come upon this Vision and are overcome
    with the dazzling sight of naked boyhood
    armpits and chest and belly and face
    that would bring Zeus to his knees—
I stare uncaring if any see me.
The boy does not open his eyes.
He could be on a hilly grassy meadow
    or inflatable raft in a blue pool
    or on his bed taking a summer nap.

I stare so long so lovingly I'm surprised
        the whole crowd doesn't turn
        to watch me staring and join
        in a staring silent circle
        around this apparition
        fallen from heaven.
The beautiful halfnaked sleeping boy Vision
        says more to me against war,
        against nuclear power, arms race,
        nationalism, imperialism, slavery,
        than all the fiery diatribes put together.
Suddenly I see the boy burn alive,
        his flesh afire writhing screaming pyre,
And the crowd melting flaming agonied forms
        from World War III's imagined holocaust reality,
And then I see him as before
        and see myself kneeling
        by his side
        as before a manger
Lavishing with ecstatic love
        my boylove dream.

# Whitmansexual

Whitman was a boysexual, a girlsexual,
    a womansexual, a mansexual,
A grasssexual, a treesexual,
    a skysexual, an earthsexual.
Whitman was an oceansexual, a mountainsexual,
    a cloudsexual, a prairiesexual,
A birdsongsexual, a lilacsmellsexual,
    a gallopinghorsesexual.
Whitman was a darknesssexual, a sleepersexual,
    a sunrisesexual, a MilkyWaysexual,
A gentlebreezesexual, an openroadsexual,
    a wildernesssexual, a democracysexual,
A drumtapssexual, a crossingbrooklynferrysexual,
    a sands-at-seventy-sexual.
Whitman was a farewell-my-fancy-sexual,
    a luckier-than-was-thought-sexual,
A deathsexual, a corpsewatchsexual,
    a compostsexual, a poets-to-come-sexual,
A miracle-sexual, an immortalitysexual,
    a cosmos-sexual, a waiting-for-you-sexual.

## Alive! Alive O!

Your heart is a cock in your chest
        that's continually ejaculating blood.
Your lungs are constantly fucking your nose
        with your breath.

# Ejaculation

Every Universe is an ejaculation!
Every sun is an ejaculation!
Every earth is an ejaculation!
Every being is an ejaculation!
Women ejaculate babies!
Girls ejaculate breasts!
Boys are ejaculations that ejaculate!
Men ejaculate six million ejaculations per orgasm!
Everyone alive ejaculates their corpse!
Everything we eat is an ejaculation!
Fruit and vegetables are ejaculations!
Trees are ejaculations—they burst up and collapse
            in a speeded-up movie of time!
Every leaf is an ejaculation!
The earth ejaculates wildflowers every spring!
The sea is a continual ejaculation!
Look at the youth surfboarding the orgasms!
Every cloud is an ejaculation!
Every lightning is an ejaculation!
Every drop of rain or snow is an ejaculation!
Every sunrise is an ejaculation!
Every waterfall is an ejaculation!
Every meteor is an ejaculation!
Every mountain is an ejaculation!
Every grain of sand is an ejaculation!
Every second that passes is an ejaculation!
This Universe has been ejaculating 100 billion years!
Scientists listen by radio telescope
            to the Big Bang's orgasmcry!
Every word spurts from our mouth!
Every book, symphony, statue, painting, film,
            house, car, plane, ship, train
            ejaculates from some brain!

Every exclamation point is an ejaculation!
Every inhalation and exhalation
        is an ejaculation!
Every shit is an ejaculation!
Every spaceship is an ejaculation!
Every nation is an ejaculation!
Every religion is an ejaculation!
Every Bible is an ejaculation!
Every Savior is an ejaculation!
I calculate ejaculate ululates through All!
Show me anything that's not an ejaculation!

## Playing It by Nose

Why playing it by ear
        when just as easily
                playing it by nose?
Why get an earful of this
        or an eyeful of that
                or a mouthful of this
        and not a noseful of that?
Why within earshot
        and not within noseshot?
Why hearsay
        and not nosesay or smellsay?
If there's an ear that eavesdrops
        why not a nose that eaves-snoops?
As the ear has an echo,
        as the eye has a mirror,
As the echo is a kind of mirror
        of the voice,
As the mirror is a kind of echo
        of the sight,
What would be an echo or a mirror
        of the smell?
If the eye with which you see God
        is the eye with which God sees you,
The nose with which you smell God
        is the nose with which
                God smells you.

# Aha!

A hundred feet under earth
      birds once flew
            a hundred feet above earth.
A hundred feet above earth
      whales once looked up a hundred feet
         to the surface of the sunny sea.

# Trees Seen Now

Trees seen now whose roots touch
        tops of trees dead centuries underground,
Someday their tops will be where roots of future trees
        will touch.

## Childfoot Visitation

One night traveling a Green Tortoise bus
      San Francisco to Seattle,
The rear of the bus converted to pads for sleeping,
Sleeping on my back as we plunged through pouring rain,
      the other weary passengers sleeping,
Suddenly something moving in my beard and under my nose
      woke me up—
Opening my eyes in the darkness
      I saw in the flickering headlight patterns
      of passing cars
The small foot of the little girl sleeping
      beside her mother.
Cleansmelling childfoot flower stretching beneath my nose
      as she changed position in her dream.
Gently pushing it away, careful not to wake her,
      I drifted off to sleep
Thinking how many men who never had a child
      are visited by a childhood foot
      slowly sliding through their beards
      opening their eyes to
      its perfect shape in the twilight?
Suddenly out of Eternity coming to me
      white and pink and smelling good,
For the first time in my life
      a little girl's naked foot
      woke me up.

# Chipmunk Crucifixion

No chipmunk had to be crucified
      on a tiny cross of twigs
To save all the other chippies,
Had to have nails pounded
      through his little paws,
Had to take upon himself
      all the sins of all the chippies
      that ever were or would be
      and die in agony
So that after they died
      all the chippies
      could live again forever,
But only if they believed
      in all the sayings and doings
      of the chipmunk crucified
      on the tiny cross of twigs.

# Lip-Licking Deer Shitting Meditation

When you become such good friends with black-tailed deer
      that live in the black oak forest
         Sierra Foothills
That 20 feet away they graze contemplating you
      as you sit on a stump in silence
         admiring them
And they think nothing of shitting in front of you
      looking over their shoulders
         across their backs and rear-ends
      their black tails lifted
As the perfectly-shaped same-size brown pellets fountain out
      in a delicate continuous fountain,
And when they gaze at you
      with their big black eyes
         while they shit
And suddenly their long pink tongues curl out
      and they're licking their lips,
Licking their lips while shitting
      and looking over at you
         with their deep shy eyes,
Isn't it proper etiquette to lick your lips back,
      to think nothing of pissing in front of them,
         showing off your cock
         and the long arc of urine
            saved up for them
         knowing they like
            its salty savor
         like salad dressing
            on their grass and mushrooms,
Isn't it proper etiquette you should look at them
      curious playful friendly
         and lick your lips in return?

# Bedrock Mortar Full Moon Illumination

Seeing the reflection of the full moon
      in the rainfilled bedrock mortar holes
            where earliest California Indians
            ground acorns with circular grinding stones
And sensing how the full moon
      is like a mortar stone in the sky,
And then seeing the image of my face
      looking up at me from the moonlit surface
        and sensing my own evanescence,
      how my face is like an acorn
        time grinds to fine dust,
And thinking thousands of years
      Indians ground acorns here
Singing their acorn songs
      gossiping and laughing
        or silent and musing
      listening to the pleasing sound
        of mortar stones grinding acorns
Or after a big storm
      gazing in the rainfilled holes
        at their reflections
      or seeing the full moon mirrored
Or deer hot from play
      dipping shy twilight muzzles
        in the cool pools
As blue oak and black oak
      ponderosa pine and digger pine
        incense cedar and manzanita
      grew and died in continuous
        ever-changing spots
      around the site.
Yet just as surely years from now
      faces staring here

After scooping out fallen leaves
    and feeling with future fingers
        the wet smooth tapering holes
    in the mossy lichen-covered rock
        contemplating themselves
    looking up at themselves
        contemplating these same thoughts
    will vanish,
While century after century the full moon
    continues to stare down
        and see its face
    unseen by anyone in the forest
Reflected in the rainfilled mortar holes
    from long ago.

# The Discovery of Lake Michigan

Canoeing down a graceful willow-lined river
        to its mouth,
Or hiking through forest parting high brush
        on some steep bluff,
Or struggling over sand dunes
        smelling water,
Suddenly the original happener-on-er
        gazing at the endless blue!

One night at twilight the first human being
        to stand on the shore of Lake Michigan
Stood on the shore of Lake Michigan
        and took a drink from a wave.
She'd never seen a body of water so big.
Perhaps this was the end of the Earth,
Perhaps this Ocean stretched on
        forever.

How many centuries passed
Before someone courageous enough
        tried canoeing across it and returned?
Whoever it was must have been regarded as
        the Columbus of Lake Michigan,
But those people didn't call it Lake Michigan
And before humans came
        Lake Michigan had no name.

## Catching the Sunrise

When I see the first light
       touch treetops on the far shore
I launch my canoe without a sound
       and float into perfect calm.
Not till the lakefloor disappears
       do I dip my paddle
And begin without a sound
       for the other side.
Not a drip or a ripple
       I go so slow.
When I reach the center of the lake
       the sun is up enough
       the far shore glows.
Soon I'm paddling in sunlight,
       mist rises in wraiths.
On seeing the bottom
       as I near the other side
I stop paddling and glide,
       not a breath of wind.
Bird sings. Fish jumps.
Looking back where I came from
       I can see the trees at my camp
       begin to be touched by the sun.

# To All Wilderness Views

Offering the View the joint,
Offering the joint the View—
          so the View can be high too,
But the View is already high,
          the View of Views.
Feasting my eyes on the View
          a zen of horizons dawns.
Do I agree with the View?
Does the View agree with me?
What are my views compared to its views?

Reviewing my life in view of the View,
I see what my prospect is from the prospect.
A prospector of prospects, my outlook is
          my vantage point, my perspective is
          my overview.
Having a Viewpoint helps in having
          a point of view—
Taking in the View,
The View takes you in too.
You're in the View and the View's in you.

## After All Is Said and Done

I want to lie down in dappled leaf-shade,
In quivering shadows of quivering leaves—
  be they oak, be they maple,
  be they elm or birch,
I want to rest in the play of shadows
   over my reclining form,
The massage of shadows
   which consoles me in its way,
Restores for me
   with whatever restoration
Flickering shadows of leaves afford—
  be they willow or aspen,
  be they poplar or beech,
I want to be caressed by shadows
   of wavering leaves,
Soothed off to sleep
   feeling the gentle breeze,
Looking up at the rustling
   sun-drenched crown—
Be it basswood, be it chestnut,
Be it walnut or hickory,
   after all is said,
   after all is done,
This is the way
I would die.

# NOTES
# AND
# INDEX

# Note on the Text

The first three parts of this five-part book were what I originally envisioned as my book titled *Last Words*. The poems in those three parts were written between 1967 and 1974. For a while I considered titling that book *First Drink From a Stream*—a title which fits it as well as *Last Words*.

"Factory," the middle part of that projected three-part book, was published as a book to itself by Lawrence Ferlinghetti's City Lights Press in 1980. It's #38 in City Lights' "Pocket Poet Series." In this present volume, "Factory" appears for the first time in the context of the other poems—from "Trying To Remember What I Learned" to "First Drink From a Stream."

Part four of this present five-part book consists of work/play meditations that elaborate and further elucidate the implications of my "Factory" poem. "Factory" was begun in 1970 and completed in 1974; it's a single, continuous poem in thirteen sections, not a collection of thirteen separate poems. "Rebecca Falls Epiphany," written in 1974, is to "Factory" what "Footnote to Howl" is to "Howl." The remaining poems in "ReWorking Work" were written between 1978 and 1983. Some of them were inspired by objections to *Factory* I had heard or read. "Winter Night Can Plant Return" is a true narrative.

The poems in part five, "Catching the Sunrise," were written between 1973 and 1983.

Therefore, this present volume *Last Words* spans 1967 to 1983.

# Notes On The Poems

### Rexroth as He Appeared to Exist . . .
—Written in 1968 after attending a party for Rexroth following his first poetry reading in Milwaukee. A sort of elegy-in-advance.

### Last Words
*Wanbli Galeshka wana ni he o who e*—Oglala Sioux for "The spotted hawk is coming to carry me away." One of the Ghost Dance songs.

"a perfect stranger by the name of Whitman"—Charles Whitman, University of Texas student who, from the 300-foot campus tower, shot and killed 14 and wounded 30 in 1966.

### Factory
Australopithecus—Early human beings who lived three million years ago in Africa.

"Even the most ethereal vision of the mystic is knowledge much as an amoeba might be said to know a man."—line from Kenneth Rexroth's long poem "The Dragon and the Unicorn."

"Engulfed Cathedral"—piano prelude by Debussy.

*Martin Eden*—great novel by Jack London I read when I was 16 and which inspired me to become writer.

*De mortuis nil nisi bonum*—Latin saying: "Speak nothing but good of the dead."

"How in 1810 the first can was made"—In 1795 Napoleon offered a prize of 12,000 francs to anyone who could come up with an effective manner of preserving food. Thousands of his soldiers were dying in battle, but even more of them were dying from starvation and food poisoning. Fourteen years later the prize was won by Nicolas Appert of Paris, a confectionary chef, pickle maker and vintner. He invented "canning" in glass jars. In 1810 Peter Durand of London applied Appert's discovery to preserving food in tin canisters.

Baluchitherium—the Earth's largest land mammal, an 18-foot-tall hornless rhinoceros that lived in Asia 20 million years ago.

Chidiock Tychborn—a 1500s youth sentenced to beheading. The only poem we have by his name is the haunting lyric he wrote the night before he died: "Lines Writ By One in the Tower, Being Young and Condemned To Die." The refrain line is "And now I live, and now my life is done." Learned this poem (also the poems of Wilfred Owen) from James Wright in the Summer of 1968.

Teratornis—an extinct carrion-eating cousin of the condor, with a wingspread of 12 feet, the largest flying bird in the history of life.

Ghost Dance—ritual dances and songs practiced by Plains Indians in the 1880s, by whose repetition they believed they could magically (without fighting) make the white man vanish, the buffalo return, and all Indians live in peace in their ancestral lands.

### Puberty of Smell
—When a friend of mine returned from Vietnam, he went back to the factory he worked in before being drafted. After his first day back on the job, he locked himself in his bedroom. His mother knocked and asked if he wanted some dinner. There was no answer. She thought he was taking a nap. Minutes later she heard the shot.

### Rebecca Falls Mescaline Epiphany
—Rebecca Falls is a tumultuous waterfall in Quetico Provincial Park, a 1750-square-mile lake-forest canoe wilderness in Ontario where I've spent more time alone than in my mother's womb and where this poem was written in October 1974.

### Written After Learning Slaves. . .
—Paul Lafargue, Karl Marx's son-in-law, in his book *La Droit à la Paresse* (*The Right To Be Lazy*), relates that slaves in ancient Greece and Rome had 115 holidays a year.

### For the Six Children Brutally Murdered by Their Father, My Cousin's Child Dead by Disease, and Walt Cieszynski Killed in Carcrash
—Wladyslaw (Walt) Cieszynski was born in Poland, lived most his life in Wisconsin. His first book of poems, *The Temple of Your Volcanic Kiss is Burning*, was about to be published by a press in San Francisco when he died at age 30 in a car crash in Milwaukee in 1976.

### Zero-Hour Day Zero-Day Workweek
—Marshall Sahlins, in his book *Stone Age Economics*, presents convincing evidence that Paleolithic people had to work only 15 hours a week

to satisfy their needs. In England in 1830 people worked 14 hours a day. A bill was introduced that would've prohibited children under 10 from working in factories and shortened the work day for those under 18 from 14 to 11½ hours. The bill was defeated on the grounds that it would "saddle the British operative with an idle, unprofitable family."

### "Your Poetry's No Good Because It Tries to Convey a Message"
—Charles Higham, in his book *Trading With The Enemy: An Exposé of the Nazi-American Money Plot 1933–49*, reveals that Standard Oil knowingly supplied fuel for German U-boats, ITT supplied communications equipment for buzz bombs that hit London, Ford maintained a factory in France that made tanks and troop carriers for the Third Reich, Chase Manhattan Bank bought and sold gold from teeth and wedding rings from death camps.

### Alan Watts Dying in His Sleep Elegy
—Two other quotes by Alan Watts to consider: "Death means going to sleep and never waking up as if we had never been born."

"To feel life is meaningless unless 'I' can be permanent is like falling desperately in love with an inch."

### Playing It by Nose
—Scientists recently discovered that salmon find their way from the Pacific Ocean back to the parent stream where they were born by the sense of smell.

### Childfoot Visitation
—occurred en route to Seattle to read at a benefit for Amnesty International in 1982. Green Tortoise is a counter-cultural alternative to Greyhound: old hippie buses piloted by authentic colorful robust veterans of the '60s.

### Chipmunk Crucifixion, Lip-Licking Deer Shitting Meditation, and Bedrock Mortar Full Moon Illumination
—were written in Fall of 1982 when I lived alone in a cabin built by Peter Orlovsky and Allen Ginsberg, near Gary Snyder's homestead in the Sierra Foothills.

### To All Wilderness Views
—As Ginsberg in *Mind Breaths* teaches a meditation on minding the breath, here I present "Mind Views," a meditation on "minding the view."

# About "Factory"

What do we do with a person who slowly tortures children to death?
That is what Factories are doing, not only to the bodies and minds
of children, but all human beings and all living things on Earth. Faster
and faster the air we breathe, water we drink, food we eat is poi-
soned by Factories. One ton of toxic substances per person in the United
States is dumped into the air, water and earth every year! The flesh
of Americans contains so much DDT it wouldn't pass federal stan-
dards for human consumption! Every day more cows, sheep and pigs
are killed in America than all the Jews in concentration camps in World
War II. Every year we use up enough trees to build a ten-foot-wide
boardwalk 30 times around the world at the equator! Each year in the
U.S. alone one million acres of oxygen-producing trees are paved over!
When Whitman heard the workers singing their varied carols he had
no idea it would be this way today. In Whitman's time Mannahatta
was smaller than Milwaukee is now. When he died in 1892, the tallest
building in Mannahatta was ten stories high.

Once people sang as they worked—songs of voyageurs, sailors, cow-
boys, harvesters with scythes. What songs do factoryworkers sing? The
workers of today don't realize they're wielding the murder weapons of
the World. They don't think eight hours a day they commit a crime
against Humanity. They don't think eight hours a day no one can be
proud working any job that contributes to Planet Death. Poets who
find themselves in Factories to survive must never forget they are spies
behind "enemy" lines, doing espionage for Humanity's Most Hope-
ful Future. What top secret will they escape with? Not for one second
should they lose sight of the fact Factories are unceasing increasing
erupting Volcanoes—supertankers moored everywhere on Earth contin-
ually spilling out death. What price do we pay for the miracle of
Factory?

In a 1971 interview, Albert Speer, Hitler's second in command, was
asked in his prison cell in Spandau: if Hitler had admitted to him
that he was exterminating the Jews, what would he have said to him.
Speer replied he would have told Hitler: "You're killing the Jews?
That is insane! I need them to work in our factories!" In the same
interview, Speer said: "It is this vast gulf between our technological
potential and our moral development that makes this age both so chal-
lenging and so terrifying. We now have the power to reach the stars—

and to destroy our own planet. . . . In a world terrorized by technology, we are *all* in Auschwitz."

I sold myself to Factory in order to make money to buy freedom to study and write Poetry! I enlisted at CCC. Not Civilian Conservation Corps, but Continental Can Company, Plant 77, one of over 200 worldwide. Surrounded by barbed wire fence, along the Milwaukee River in Milwaukee, Wisconsin: the largest can factory in the world under one roof. I worked in the press dept., packaging the tops and bottoms of cans into narrow bags or cardboard tubes as they came from a machine called a press which punched them from sheets of aluminum. The press machines were like huge machine guns except rather than shooting bullets they shot lids—1000 a minute advancing toward me in a column down a long narrow chute. Once packaged, the lids were shipped by fork-lift trucks called hysters to the other side of the dept., where they were run through machines called minsters. The sole purpose of the minsters, each of which cost half a million dollars, was to stamp fliptops onto the lids. The minsters were even louder than the presses. Each new worker had his ears measured and was given a set of earplugs in a carrying case and was expected to wear them at all times on the job. They helped, but only somewhat. When you lay in bed waiting to fall asleep, the sound of the machines would still be ringing in your ears as loud as if two shells were put next to them and you were hearing the sea. Two months after I quit, the machines still ringing in my ears, I sat down with notes I'd written on the job and began arranging and expanding them into the 13 sections of "Factory."

I hear an empty can blown clattering down the alley in the wind. I remember those sweltering months in the bowels of the Factory. Thousands of poets (perhaps millions) are working in Factories as I write this. May poems more powerful and tender than I'll ever write leap from their brains! May they inspire others and may those others inspire others! May we live to see a time when it seems the world is not doomed, a time when each human enlightenment is worth more than all the money in the world!

# Index of Titles

# The Antler'd Dancer

The antler'd dancer is a prehistoric painting on a ceiling which domi-
nates the innermost recesses of Les Trois Frères cave in Ariège, France.
The cave, in the Pyrenees, was discovered a few days before World
War I by three boys who were brothers. Inside a grotto they found
a long tubelike passage—a flume, hardly two feet in diameter—through
which one had to crawl and wriggle on one's belly for 50 yards to
come to a large chamber with animal forms engraved everywhere on
the walls. Above them, facing the mouth of the difficult passage, on
the ceiling 15 feet from floor level in a craggy rocky apse, watching,
peering at the visitor with penetrating eyes, is the antler'd dancer
(29½ inches high and 15 inches across, engraved and bearing black paint),
who has the appearance of a man with the horns of a stag, eyes of
an owl, ears of a deer, paws of a bear, tail of a horse, and who is plainly
dancing or prancing.

adapted from *The Masks of God: Primitive Mythology* by Joseph Campbell

Figures of men wearing antlers on their heads reveal something of
the way the Paleolithic mind worked. The so-called Sanctuary of Les
Trois Frères is a bell-shaped alcove with overhanging rocks and fis-
sures. At the top of the "bell," we find engraved and painted the fa-
mous figure of the "Sorcerer" which the Abbé Breuil called "the Horned
God." This composite being presides over the "Sanctuary" of the cave,
whose walls are crowded with the most remarkable animal figures: bi-
son, mammoth, rhinoceros, lion, bear, ibex, horse. The "Sorcerer" has
the appearance of a man bending forward, his eyes big and round like
those of a night bird or a lion or a "ghost," deer antlers on his head,
and the ears and shoulders of a stag. The lower part of the back is
provided with a horse's tail, below which the sexual parts are seen,
rather human in shape, but located where a feline's would be. The Abbé
Breuil interprets the figure as "the god of Les Trois Frères, the arch
sorcerer embodying the attributes and exercising the functions of all
the creatures he depicts, the spirit governing hunting expeditions and
the propagation of game." It is not surprising to find so hypersymbolic
a figure at the highest and innermost point of a chamber that is dec-

orated with hundreds of figures, in the arrangement of which Magdalenian symbolism is displayed with a richness unattained elsewhere."

from *Treasures of Prehistoric Art* by André Leroi-Gourhan

---

One of the oldest drawings of a shaman that we have is the famous "Dancing Sorcerer" in the late Old Stone Age cave of Trois Frères in southern France—a man dressed up in the skins of various animals that were hunted for food, and over which his ritual dance had power. It is interesting that the Sorcerer wears a headdress of deer antlers, because deer antlers in some species seem to act as a stimulus that attracts other deer closer for combat and thus to be killed by hunters. This biological fact would seem to account for the persistent prevalence of deer antlers in hunting magic—all the way from Mesolithic Star Carr in southern England and the deer-horned Gallic divinity Cernunnus who lingered in southern France until Roman times, to the deer-antlered shamans of central Siberia still known to anthropologists in the 18th century, to the sacred antlered kings of ancient Iran and archaic China (where animal horns are still valued in magic and medicine), and indeed even to Central America where deer-magic is still closely related symbolically to the ritual hallucinogenic cactus, peyote.

from "Shamanic Origins of Religion and Medicine" by Weston La Barre, Ph.D. in *Journal of Psychedelic Drugs*, Vol. 11, 1979